head to toe knits

head to toe knits

35 hats, scarves, gloves, and socks you'll ♥ to knit

Bronwyn Lowenthal

Additional projects by Melody Griffiths

CICO BOOKS

LONDON NEW YORK

Published in 2010 by CICO Books
An imprint of Ryland Peters & Small Ltd

20–21 Jockey's Fields   519 Broadway, 5th Floor
London WC1R 4BW   New York, NY 10012

www.cicobooks.com

10 9 8 7 6 5 4 3 2 1

Text © Bronwyn Lowenthal and Melody Griffiths 2010
Design and photography © CICO Books 2010

A CIP catalog record for this book is available from the Library of
Congress and the British Library.

ISBN-13: 978 1 907030 64 2

Printed in China

Editor: Kate Haxell
Designer: Louise Leffler
Photographer: Becky Maynes, Tino Tedaldi, and Dygo Uetsuji

Love Lowie, love knitting
www.ilovelowie.com

Contents

introduction

When I was asked to write this, my third book, I wanted to concentrate on projects that are both fashionably desirable and very wearable for a broad cross-section of knit-lovers. Meeting customers in my Lowie shop in Covent Garden, London, and through my online boutique at www.ilovelowie.com, I've been getting a good idea of what knit-lovers want to wear and I hope that this book gives you some great projects to sink your needles into.

In my first book, **Love to Knit**, I was inspired by "granny chic"—vintage styling for fashion-lovers. My second book, **Love to Knit Socks**, was true to its title and full of gorgeous socks, stylish legwarmers, and cozy slippers. Of the 35 projects in **Head to Toe Knits**, I've dedicated plenty of pages to fashion-forward, big, chunky scarves and hope that you'll embrace the volume in those projects. I've also included favorite projects—as recommended by you—from my first two books: how wonderful that some of you visited the shop to show me finished projects you'd knitted from those books.

I often get emails asking for patterns from my Lowie boutique mainline knit collection. In this book I've included two such projects; a fantastically long and chunky giant cable scarf which knits up beautifully in pure wool Aran yarn (page 44) and the reversible check and stripe wrap (page 30). The wrap's reversibility is absolute genius, inspired by a talented granny.

Some of my other favorite projects are the cute bobble wristwarmers (page 54), the peaked ribbed beanie (page 14), and the sparkly legwarmers (page 80). If you're a novice knitter, there are straightforward instructions to start you off (page 98 onward) and you'll find some easy beginner's projects to make; the simple snood (page 34), string bag (page 94), and armwarmers (page 50) will also make great presents. For those who like a challenge, try knitting the cozy Turkish socks (page 68) or lacy shawl (page 40).

We all knit with a unique "hand" and have our own ideas of colors and yarns, so I encourage you to embrace your own creativity and I look forward to seeing your finished projects from **Head to Toe Knits**.

Bronwyn Lowenthal

heads up

embellished beret

If you only knit one hat, this beret is the one to make—it will give any outfit instant chic. Customize and personalize your beret by adding buttons or bows instead of vintage lace. Berets don't have to be worn at a jaunty angle, Parisian-artist-style: they're very cute tugged down to cover your ears or pulled back to show your hairline.

Size
To fit average-size adult head

Yarn suggestion
One 3½oz (100g) ball—approximately 126yds (115m)—of chunky-weight yarn, such as Rowan Cocoon

Needles
Pair of US 11 (8.0mm) knitting needles

Other materials
Knitter's sewing needle
Pieces of vintage lace
Sewing needle and thread

Gauge (tension)
12 stitches and 18 rows to 4in (10cm) square over st st using US 11 (8.0mm) needles

Abbreviations
See page 101

pattern
Cast on 54 sts.
Row 1: *K1, p1, rep from * to end.
Rep row 1 twice more.
Row 4 (RS): *K1, inc, rep from * to end. *81 sts*
Row 5: Purl.
Row 6: K4, *inc, k7, rep from * to last 5 sts, inc, k4. *91 sts*
Row 7 and foll 2 alt rows: Purl.
Row 8: K5, *inc, k8, rep from * to last 5 sts, inc, k4. *101 sts*
Row 10: K6, *inc, k9, rep from * to last 5 sts, inc, k4. *111 sts*
Row 12: K7, *inc, k10, rep from * to last 5 sts, inc, k4. *121 sts*
Row 13: Purl.
Row 14: Knit.
Row 15: Purl.
Rep rows 14–15 twice more.

Shape crown
Row 20: K7, *k2tog, k10, rep from * to last 6 sts, k2tog, k4. *111 sts*
Row 21 and foll 8 alt rows: Purl.
Row 22: K6, *k2tog, k9, rep from * to last 6 sts, k2tog, k4. *101 sts*
Row 24: K5, *k2tog, k8, rep from * to last 6 sts, k2tog, k4. *91 sts*
Row 26: K4, *k2tog, k7, rep from * to last 6 sts, k2tog, k4. *81 sts*
Row 28: K3, *k2tog, k6, rep from * to last 6 sts, k2tog, k4. *71 sts*
Row 30: K2, *k2tog, k5, rep from * to last 6 sts, k2tog, k4. *61 sts*
Row 32: K1, *k2tog, k4, rep from * to last 6 sts, k2tog, k4. *51 sts*
Row 34: *K2tog, k3, rep from * to last 6 sts, k2tog, k4. *41 sts*
Row 36: *K2, k2tog, rep from * to last st, k1. *31 sts*
Row 38: *K1, k2tog, rep from * to last st, k1. *21 sts*
Row 39: *P2tog, rep from * to last st, p1. *11 sts*
Break yarn, thread through rem 11 sts, pull up tightly and secure.

FINISHING
Sew seam neatly. Position the pieces of lace on your beret and when you are happy with the look, sew them in place.

cloche hat

A cool pattern that's easy to knit, dogtooth check works really well with this casual hat style. It's knitted here in classic black and white, but you could try two vivid colors for a completely different feel.

pattern

CROWN
Using A, cast on 66 sts.
Row 1: Knit.
Row 2: Purl.
Row 3: Knit.
Row 4: Knit.
Change to B.
Row 5: K2, *sl 1, K3, rep from * to end.
Row 6: P3, *sl 1, p3, rep from * to last 3 sts, sl 1, p2.
Row 7: As row 5.
Row 8: Knit.
Change to A.
Row 9: K4, *sl 1, k3, rep from * to last 2 sts, sl 1, k1.
Row 10: P1, *. sl 1, p3, rep from * to last st, p1.
Row 11: As row 9.
Row 12: Knit.
Rep rows 5–12 twice more, then rep rows 5–6 again.
Shape crown
Cont in B.
Row 31: K2, *k2tog, k2, rep from * to end. *50 sts*
Row 32: P1, *p2tog, p1, rep from * to last st, p1. *34 sts*
Row 33: *K2tog, rep from * to end. *17 sts*
Row 34: *P2tog, rep from * to last st, p1. *9 sts*
Break yarn, thread through rem sts and pull up tight.

BRIM
Using B, cast on 10 sts.
Row 1: Knit.
Row 2: Knit.
Row 3: K7, turn, k to end.
Row 4: Knit across all sts.
Rep rows 2–4 until when slightly stretched shorter edge of brim fits around cast on edge of hat.
Bind (cast) off.

FINISHING
Weave in yarn ends. Sew back seam of hat. Sew shorter edge of brim to cast on edge of hat.

Size
To fit average-size adult head

Yarn suggestion
One 3½oz (100g) ball—approximately 126yds (115m)—of chunky-weight yarn, such as Rowan Cocoon, in white (A), and two balls—approximately 252yds (230m)—in black (B)

Needles
Pair of US 13 (9.0mm) knitting needles

Other materials
Knitter's sewing needle

Gauge (tension)
15 stitches and 23 rows to 4in (10cm) square over patt using US 13 (9.0mm) needles

Abbreviations
See page 101

Note: slip all sts purlwise to avoid twisting them.

peaked ribbed beanie

The shape of this modern and practical hat means you can pull it down over your ears to keep you cozy on cold days. I love the soft peak, which can be worn straight at the front or on a slight angle.

Size
To fit average-size adult head

Yarn suggestion
Two 3½oz (100g) balls—approximately 126yds (170m)—of worsted-weight yarn, such as Rowan Pure Wool Aran

Needles
Set of four double-pointed US 6 (4.0mm) knitting needles
Set of four double-pointed US 7 (4.5mm) knitting needles
Pair of US 6 (4.0mm) knitting needles

Other materials
Knitter's sewing needle
US E4 (3.5mm) crochet hook
Length of shirring elastic

Gauge (tension)
19 stitches and 25 rows to 4in (10cm) square over st st using US 7 (4.5mm) needles

Abbreviations
See page 101

pattern

BEANIE
Using US 6 (4.0mm) double-pointed needles cast on 91 sts.
Distribute these sts evenly over 3 of the double-pointed needles and place a round marker after the last st.
Using 4th needle, work in rounds as folls:
Round 1 (RS): *K4, p3, rep from * to end.
Rep last round ten more times.
Change to US 7 (4.5mm) needles.
Round 12: *K4, inc once purlwise in each of next 2 sts, p1, rep from * to end. *117 sts*
Rounds 13 and 14: *K4, p5, rep from * to end.
Round 15: *K4, inc purlwise in next st, p2, inc purlwise in next st, p1, rep from * to end. *143 sts*

Rounds 16 to 32: *K4, p7, rep from * to end.
Round 33: *K4, p2tog, p3, p2tog tbl, rep from * to end. *117 sts*
Round 34 to 36: *K4, p5, rep from * to end.
Round 37: *K4, p2tog, p1, p2tog tbl, rep from * to end. *91 sts*
Round 38 to 40: *K4, p3, rep from * to end.
Round 41: *K1, k2tog, k1, p2tog, p1, rep from * to end. *65 sts*
Rounds 42 to 44: *K3, p2, rep from * to end.
Round 45: *K1, k2tog, p2tog, rep from * to end. *39 sts*
Rounds 46 and 47: *K2, p1, rep from * to end.
Round 48: *K2tog, p1, rep from * to end. *26 sts*
Rounds 49 and 50: *K1, p1, rep from * to end.
Round 51: *K2tog tbl, rep from * to end. *13 sts*
Round 52: K13.
Break yarn and thread through rem 13 sts. Pull up tight and fasten off securely.

PEAK
Using US 6 (4.0mm) needles cast on 60 sts.
Row 1 (RS): K44, wrap next st and turn.
Row 2: K28, wrap next st and turn.
Row 3: K30, wrap next st and turn.
Row 4: K32, wrap next st and turn.
Row 5: K34, wrap next st and turn.
Row 6: K36, wrap next st and turn.
Row 7: K38, wrap next st and turn.
Cont in this way, working 2 more sts on every row before wrapping next st and turning, until the foll row has been worked:
Row 16 (WS): K56, wrap next st and turn.
Row 17: Knit to end.
Using a US 7 (4.5mm) needle, cast off all sts loosely knitwise.

FINISHING
Do NOT press.
Cut length of shirring elastic to fit snugly around head and join ends. Using US E4 (3.5mm) crochet hook, attach yarn to cast-on edge of beanie and work 1 round of single (double) crochet around cast-on edge, enclosing shirring elastic in sts.
Sew cast-on edge of peak to front of beanie as in photograph.

sequined earmuffs

Add instant retro charm to any outfit with these sweet earmuffs, which have the added benefit of keeping your ears cozy on the coldest days. Choose felted wool or lightweight fleece to line the earmuffs and satin ribbon to tie under your chin or at the nape of your neck.

Size
To fit average-size adult head

Yarn suggestion
One 3½oz (100g) ball—approximately 126yds (115m)—of chunky-weight yarn, such as Rowan Cocoon

Needles
Pair of US 11 (8.0mm) knitting needles

Other materials
Knitter's sewing needle
18 x 4in (45 x 10cm) piece of felted wool or fleece fabric
Fabric marker
Scissors
Sewing needle and thread to match yarn
Approximately 100 silver sequins
Pink sewing thread
Two 32in (80cm) lengths of ⅝-in (1.5-cm) wide pink satin ribbon

Gauge (tension)
12 stitches and 18 rows to 4in (10cm) square over st st using US 11 (8.0mm) needles

Abbreviations
See page 101

pattern

ONE EARMUFF (make 2)
Cast on 2 sts.
Row 1: Knit.
Row 2: K1, m1, k1.
Row 3: K1, p1, k1.
Row 4: K1, m1, k1, m1, k1.
Row 5: K1, p3, k1.
Row 6: K1, m1, k to last st, m1, k1.
Row 7: K1, p to last st, k1.
Rep rows 6–7 three more times. *13 sts*
Row 14: K1, skpo, k to last 3 sts, k2tog, k1.
Work 3 rows.
Rep the last 4 rows once more.
Rep row 14 once more. *7 sts*
Work 5 rows.
Row 28: K1, skpo, k to last 3 sts, k2tog, k1.
Work 9 rows st st.
Bind (cast) off.

FINISHING
Sew bound (cast) off edges together. Press according to yarn ball band. Sew a length of ribbon to the point of each earmuff. Right-side down, lay the knitting on the felt and draw around it with the fabric marker. Cut out the shape. Turning under ¼-in (5mm) all around and using the sewing needle and matching thread, blanket stitch the felt to the back of the knitting, covering the ends of the ribbon. Following the photograph, sew a spiral of sequins to each earmuff (see page 125), joining them with a line of sequins across the straight section.

fair isle earflap hat

This is a good Fair Isle project for color-knitting novices as it's worked in the round—so the right side is always facing you and you can see where you are in the pattern—and you are only ever using two colors at a time. It's an easy-to-wear hat style that suits most faces and you can get creative with your color palette.

Size
To fit average-size adult head

Yarn suggestion
Approximately 4½:5½oz (120:150g) of wool and wool-mix sport-weight yarn; about 2½:3oz (70:85g) of this should be in the main color (A), and 2:2½oz (50:65g) in contrasting colors (B)

Needles
One US 6 (4.0mm) circular knitting needle, 24in (61cm) long
Set of four double-pointed US 6 (4.0mm) knitting needles
One US 3 (3.25mm) circular needle, 32in (81cm) long

Other materials
Knitter's sewing needle

Gauge (tension)
24 stitches and 26 rows to 4in (10cm) over Fair Isle patt using US 6 (4.0mm) needles

Abbreviations
See page 101

Note: the chart does not show any changes of color in the contrasting color (B). Change these B colors whenever you wish. Spread out the stitches on the right-hand needle each time you change color. This will stop the color rounds from pulling in.

If you haven't done any Fair Isle knitting before, then this is a great project to try.

pattern

CROWN

Using US 6 (4.0mm) circular needle and A, cast on 132(144) sts.
Place a round marker after the last st. Work in rounds as folls:

Round 1: Knit.

Work in patt from chart on page 21, changing to double-pointed needles when necessary.

Round 2: Omit edge st, rep 12 sts of first line of chart eleven:twelve times.

This round sets chart patt.

Cont in patt from chart, changing colors for B whenever you desire, and work 34 more rounds from chart.

Beg with 8th line of chart, work 20 rounds from chart.

Dec round 1: Using A, [k9:10, k2tog] 12 times. *120:132 sts*

Beg with first line of chart, patt 7 rounds.

K 1 round in A.

Dec round 2: [K8:9, k2tog] twelve times. *108:120 sts*

K 1 round.

Dec round 3: [K7:8, k2tog] twelve times. *96:108 sts*

K 1 round.

Dec round 4: [K6:7, k2tog] twelve times. *84:96 sts*

K 1 round.

Dec round 5: [K5:6, k2tog] twelve times. *72:84 sts*

K 1 round.

Dec round 6: [K4:5, k2tog] twelve times. *60:72 sts*

K 1 round.

Dec round 7: [K3:4, k2tog] twelve times. *48:60 sts*
K 1 round.
Dec round 8: [K2:3, k2tog] twelve times. *36:48 sts*
K 1 round.
Dec round 9: [K1:2, k2tog] twelve times. *24:36 sts*
K 1 round.
2nd size only
Dec round 10: [K1, k2tog] twelve times.
K 1 round.
Both sizes 24 sts
Next round: [K2tog] 12 times. *12 sts*
K 1 round.
Next round: [K2tog] 6 times. *6 sts*
Leaving a long end, cut yarn. Thread end through sts, draw up, and secure top of hat.

EARFLAPS
RIGHT EARFLAP
With RS facing, skip 17:20 sts from start of round 1.
Using 2 of the double-pointed needles and A, pick up 17 sts from next 17 sts of cast on edge of hat.
Row 1: Purl.
Work in patt from chart, as folls:
Row 2 (RS): K2A, reading 14th line of chart as a k row from right to left, work edge st and 12 sts of repeat, k2A.
Row 3: P2A, reading 15th line of chart as a p row, work 12 sts of repeat and edge st, p2A.
These 2 rows set chart patt in rows.
Cont in patt, work 7 more rows.
Row 11: Purl.
Row 12 (dec row) (RS): K1, [k2tog] twice, k to last 5 sts, [skpo] twice, k1. *13 sts*
Row 13: Purl.
Row 14: As row 12. *9 sts*
Row 15: Purl.
Bind (cast) off.

LEFT EARFLAP
With RS facing, skip 65:71 sts.
Using 2 of the double-pointed needles and A, pick up 17 sts from next 17 sts of cast on edge of hat.
Complete as given for Right Earflap.

EDGING
Using US 3 (3.25mm) circular needle and A, with RS facing, beg at start of Round 1 of hat, pick up 17:20 sts to right earflap, 29 sts around earflap, 65:71 sts to left earflap, 29 sts around left earflap and 16:19 sts to beg of round. *156:168 sts*
Round 1: [P1, k1] to end.
This round forms rib. Rib 3 more rounds.
Turn the work and bind (cast) off loosely purlwise.

FINISHING
Weave in yarn ends. Press hat. Make a 5in (13cm) tassel in one of the B shades and sew to top of hat.

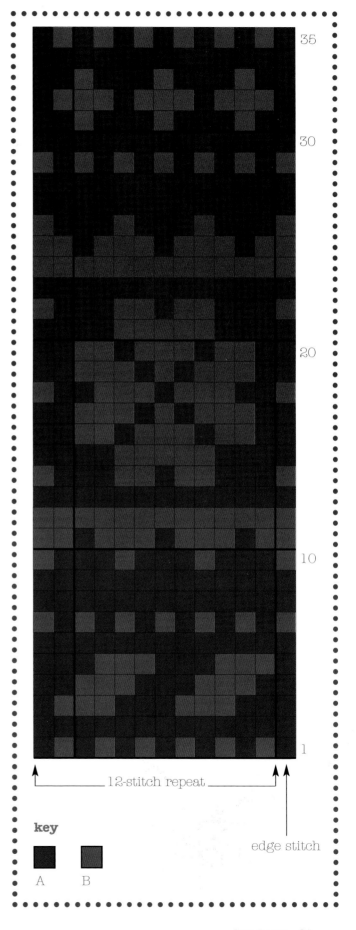

35
30
20
10
1

12-stitch repeat

edge stitch

key

A   B

lacy beanie

White yarn and pale cream lace give this pretty beanie a vintage feel that complements the easy-to-knit lace pattern. However, you can try a bold color lace for an eye-catching accent, or contrast colors of yarn and lace for a very different look.

pattern

Using 2 strands of yarn held together, cast on 101 sts.

Knit 1 row.

Now work in lace patt as folls:

Row 1: K2tog, *k3, yo, k1, yo, k3, sk2po, rep from * to last 9 sts, k3, yo, k1, yo, k3, skpo.

Row 2 and every foll alt row: Purl.

Row 3: K2tog, *k2, yo, k3, yo, k2, sk2po, rep from * to last 9 sts, k2, yo, k3, yo, k2, skpo.

Row 5: K2tog, *k1, yo, k5, yo, k1, sk2po, rep from * to last 9 sts, k1, yo, k5, yo, k1, skpo.

Row 7: K2tog, *yo, k7, yo, sk2po, rep from * to last 9 sts, yo, k7, yo, skpo.

Row 8: Purl.

These 8 rows form lace patt.

Rep last 8 rows four more times.

Next row: K1, *k3, k2tog, rep from * to end. *81 sts*

Next row: Purl.

Next row: K1, *k2, k2tog, rep from * to end. *61 sts*

Next row: Purl.

Next row: K1, *k1, k2tog, rep from * to end. *41 sts*

Next row: Purl.

Next row: K1, *k2tog, rep from * to end. *21 sts*

Next row: Purl.

Break yarn and thread through rem 21 sts. Pull up tight and fasten off securely.

FINISHING

Sew back seam. Coil the lace up like a snail, stitching the bottom edge to the back of the previous coil as you go to make a rosette. Stitch the rosette to the side of the beanie.

Size

To fit small to medium adult head

Yarn suggestion

One ¾oz (25g) ball—approximately 229yds (210m)—of fine kid mohair yarn, such as Rowan Kidsilk Haze

Needles

Pair of US 6 (4.0mm) knitting needles

Other materials

Knitter's sewing needle
28in (70cm) of ½-in (12-mm) wide lace
Sewing needle and thread

Gauge (tension)

23 stitches and 32 rows to 4in (10cm) square over lace patt using 2 strands of yarn held together and US 6 (4.0mm) needles

Abbreviations

See page 101

keep cozy

maxi scarf with pockets

This super-large scarf is big enough to be used as a wrap. The cute snowflake-design patch pockets in a different-textured yarn create a nice contrast detail, and will keep your hands warm, too.

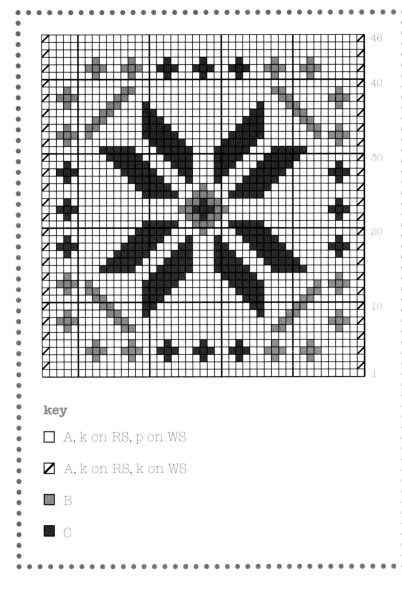

key

☐ A, k on RS, p on WS

◩ A, k on RS, k on WS

▨ B

■ C

Size
Approximately 78¾in (200cm) long and approx 13¾in (35cm) wide.

Yarn suggestion
Ten 3½oz (100g) balls—approximately 875yds (800m)—of bulky-weight yarn, such as Gedifra Highland Alpaca, in grey (MC)
One 1¾oz (50g) ball—approximately 191yds (175m)—of sport-weight yarn, such as Rowan Felted Tweed, in each of light gray (A), ginger (B), and dark gray (C)

Needles
Pair of US 15 (10.0mm) knitting needles
Pair of US 5 (3.75mm) knitting needles

Other materials
Knitter's sewing needle

Gauge (tension)
9 stitches and 12½ rows to 4in (10cm) square over st st using US 15 (10.0mm) needles and Big Wool
23 stitches and 32 rows to 4in (10cm) square over st st using US 5 (3.75mm) needles and Felted Tweed

Abbreviations
See page 101

pattern

SCARF

Using US 15 (10.0mm) needles and MC, cast on 31 sts.

Row 1 (RS): K2, [p1, k1] fourteen times, k1.

Row 2: K1, [p1, k1] fifteen times.

These 2 rows form rib.

Work in rib for a further 4 rows.

Row 7: Knit.

Row 8: K1, p29, k1.

Rep last 2 rows until scarf measures 76¾in (195cm), ending with a WS row.

Now work in rib for 6 rows.

Bind (cast) off in rib.

POCKETS (MAKE 2)

Using US 5 (3.75mm) needles and A, cast on 45 sts.

Using a separate ball of yarn for each block of color, work 46 rows from chart, ending with a WS row.

Break off A and C and cont using B only.

Next row (RS): K2, *p1, k1, rep from * to last st, k1.

Next row: K1, *p1, k1, rep from * to end.

Rep last 2 rows three more times.

Bind (cast) off in rib.

FINISHING

Weave in yarn ends. Press according to yarn ball band.

Using photograph as a guide, sew pockets onto ends of scarf, approximately 5 rows above rib.

If color knitting seems a bit too complicated, just knit the basic scarf; you'll love its huge size.

The beehive texture
is only an eight-row
pattern, so it's
really easy to knit.

beehive scarf

A seriously chunky scarf to snuggle into in winter weather. The textured beehive pattern isn't at all difficult to knit and once you've established the rhythm of the pattern, it'll flow easily off your needles.

pattern

Cast on 25 sts.

Row 1: Knit.

Row 2: Knit to last st, pick up loop lying between needles and place this loop on right needle (this loop does NOT count as a st), slip last st knitwise.

Row 3: K tog the first st and the picked-up loop, knit to last st, pick up loop lying between needles and place this loop on right needle (this loop does NOT count as a st), slip last st knitwise.

Rows 4–6: As row 3.

Keeping first and last 3 sts correct as set by first 6 rows, now work center 19 sts in beehive patt as folls:

Row 1: Patt 3 sts, [sl 1, k3] four times, sl 1, k2, patt 3 sts.

Row 2: Patt 3 sts, p2, sl 1, [p3, sl 1] four times, patt 3 sts.

Rows 3–4: Patt 3 sts, p19, patt 3 sts.

Row 5: Patt 3 sts, k2, sl 1, [k3, sl 1] four times, patt 3 sts.

Row 6: Patt 3 sts, [sl 1, p3] four times, sl 1, p2, patt 3 sts.

Rows 7–8: Patt 3 sts, p19, patt 3 sts.

These 8 rows form beehive patt.

Cont as set until scarf measures approximately 70in (180cm), ending after beehive patt row 3 or 7.

Next row: K tog the first st and the picked-up loop, knit to last st, pick up loop lying between needles and place this loop on right needle (this loop does NOT count as a st), slip last st knitwise.

Rep this row four more times.

Bind (cast) off.

FINISHING

Cut 44 lengths of yarn, each 16in (40cm) long, and knot each length through a cast on or bound (cast) off stitch to form fringes on each end of the scarf.

Size

7½in (19cm) wide and 70in (180cm) long, excluding fringe

Yarn suggestion

Nine 1¾oz (50g) balls—approximately 413yds (378m)—of bulky-weight yarn, such as Debbie Bliss Como

Needles

Pair of US 13 (9.0mm) knitting needles

Gauge (tension)

13 stitches and 20 rows to 4in (10cm) square over beehive patt using US 13 (9.0mm) needles

Abbreviations

See page 101

reversible check and stripe wrap

My reversible wrap is check on one side and stripy on the other so that you can play around with how you wear it. In our photos we've styled it with a section of the stripe turned back and pinned for pattern contrast. Bright colors will produce a younger fashion look, while more muted colors will be classic and versatile.

Size
Approximately 73in (185cm) along longest edge and 26in (66cm) wide.

Yarn suggestion
Ten 1¾oz (50g) balls—approximately 1260yds (1150m)—of sport-weight yarn, such as Rowan Cocoon, in each of pink (A) and aubergine (B)

Needles
Pair of US 10 (6.0mm) knitting needles

Other materials
Knitter's sewing needle
Decorative kilt pin

Gauge (tension)
16 stitches and 27 rows to 4in (10cm) square over patt using US 10 (6.0mm) needles and 3 strands of yarn held together

Abbreviations
See page 101
Note: slip sts purlwise to avoid twisting them

pattern

FIRST SECTION
**Using 3 strands of A held together, cast on 105 sts.
Row 1 (WS): [P1, k1] to last st, p1.
Row 2: K1, [p1, k1] to end.
Row 3: As row 1.
Join in 3 strands of B held together and now work in patt as folls:
Row 4 (RS): With B, k4, *sl1 with yarn at back (WS) of work, k3, rep from * to last st, k1.
Row 5: With B, k4, *sl1 with yarn at front (WS) of work, p3, rep from * to last 5 sts, sl1 with yarn at front (WS) of work, k4.
Row 6: With B, k4, *sl1 with yarn at back (WS) of work, k3, rep from * to last st, k1.
Row 7: With A, k6, *sl1 with yarn at back (RS) of work, k3, rep from * to last 3 sts, k3.
Row 8: With A, k6, *sl1 with yarn at back (WS) of work, k3, rep from * to last 3 sts, k3.
Row 9: With A, k4, p2, *sl1 with yarn at front (WS) of work, p3, rep from * to last 7 sts, sl1 with yarn at front (WS) of work, p2, k4.
Row 10: As row 8.
Row 11: With B, k4, *sl1 with yar at back (RS), k3, rep from * to last st, k1.
Rows 4–11 form patt.
Cont in patt until first section measures 23½in (67cm), ending with a RS row.**
Break yarn and leave sts on a holder.

SECOND SECTION
Work as given for First Section from ** to **.

JOIN SECTIONS
Next row (WS): Patt 105 sts of second section, place marker on needle, then patt 105 sts of first section. 210 sts
Keeping patt correct, now shape point as folls:
Next row (RS): Patt to within 3 sts of marker, k3tog, slip marker onto right needle, sk2po, patt to end. 206 sts
Next row: Patt to within 2 sts of marker, p2tog tbl, slip marker onto right needle, p2tog, patt to end. 204 sts
Rep last 2 rows 33 times more. 6 sts
Next row: K3tog, sk2po.
Next row: P2tog and fasten off.

FINISHING
Weave in yarn ends. Press according to yarn ball band.
Fasten fronts with kilt pin as in photograph.

roll-neck capelet

A sophisticated variation on a scarf, this ribbed capelet sits neatly over your shoulders and the deep roll-neck is deliciously snug. Wear it as a warm cover-up over a dress or top in the evening, or over a form-fitting jacket.

Size
Approximately 45½in (116cm) around lower edge and 8½in (22cm) long excluding collar

Yarn suggestion
Three 3½oz (100g) balls—approximately 360yds (330m)—of chunky-weight yarn, such as Rowan British Sheep Breeds Undyed

Needles
One US 10½ (7.0mm) circular needle, 24in (60cm) long

Other materials
Knitter's sewing needle

Gauge (tension)
12 stitches and 18 rows to 4in (10cm) over rib in the round, when pressed, on US 10½ (7.0mm) circular needle

Abbreviations
See page 101

pattern

Cast on 140 sts.
Place a round marker after the last st.
Work in rounds as folls:
Round 1 (RS): [K2, p2] to end, joining sts into a round.
This round forms rib.
Rib 35 more rounds.
Dec round 1: [K2, p1, k2tog, skpo, p1, k2, rib 10] 7 times. *126 sts*
Dec round 2: [K2, k2tog, skpo, k2, rib 10] 7 times. *112 sts*
Dec round 3: [K1, k2tog, skpo, k1, rib 10] 7 times. *98 sts*
Dec round 4: [K2tog, skpo, rib 10] 7 times. *84 sts*
Rib 44 rounds to form roll-neck collar.
Bind (cast) off in rib.

FINISHING
Weave in yarn ends. Press according to yarn ball band.

simple snood

So easy and very quick to knit, this snood doesn't need much yarn either—an ideal project! Keep it tucked in your bag for when you need that extra bit of warmth: it fills the chilly gap between your coat collar and chin perfectly. Pulled up over your hair it also makes a great earwarmer or headband for really cold days.

This is such a speedy project to knit, and such a great accessory to own; make lots of them in colors to match all your winter outfits.

pattern

Cast on 75 sts.
Distribute these sts evenly over 3 of the double-pointed needles and place a round marker after the last st.
Using 4th needle, work in rounds as folls:
Rounds 1–2: Knit.
Round 3: *K3, yo, k2tog, rep from * to end.
Rep these 3 rounds thirteen more times, then rep rounds 1 and 2 again.
Bind (cast) off.

FINISHING
Weave in yarn ends. Press according to yarn ball band.

Size
Approximately 22in (55cm) diameter and 9in (23cm) deep
• •
Yarn suggestion
Two 1¾oz (50g) balls—approximately 192yds (176m)—of bulky-weight yarn, such as ggh Davos
• •
Needles
Set of four double-pointed US 10 (6.0mm) knitting needles
• •
Other materials
Round marker
Knitter's sewing needle
• •
Gauge (tension)
13.5 stitches and 20 rows to 4in (10cm) square over lace patt using US 10 (6.0mm) needles
• •
Abbreviations
See page 101
• •

sparkly ripple scarf

The contrast between the metallic yarn and soft wool adds to the rippled texture of this slim scarf. The scarf has pointed ends, giving a neck-tie effect, and the sparkly yarn is ideal for evenings out.

Size
Approximately 70in (177.5cm) long and approx 5in (12.5cm) wide

Yarn suggestion
Three ¾oz (25g) balls—approximately 574yds (525m)—of metallic yarn, such as Rowan Shimmer (A)
One 1¾oz (50g) ball—approximately 175yds (160m)—of fingering-weight yarn, such as Rowan Cashsoft 4 ply (B)

Needles
Pair of US 6 (4.0mm) knitting needles

Other materials
Knitter's sewing needle

Gauge (tension)
22 stitches and 30 rows to 4in (10cm) square over patt using US 6 (4.0mm) needles.

Abbreviations
m1k = make one st by picking up loop between needles and knitting into back of this loop.
m1p = make one st by picking up loop between needles and purling into back of this loop.
See also page 101

pattern

Using A and B held together cast on 39 sts.
Row 1 (RS): With A and B held together, knit.
Row 2: With A and B held together, k3, m1k, k31, k2tog, k3.
Rows 3–6: As rows 1–2, twice.
Row 7: With A and B held together, knit.
Row 8: With A and B held together, k3, m1p, p31, p2tog, k3.
Row 9: As row 7.
Row 10: With A only, k3, m1p, p31, p2tog, k3.
Row 11: With A only, k4, [yfwd, k2tog] 16 times, k3.
Rows 12 and 13: As rows 10–11.
Row 14: As row 8.
Rows 15–16: As rows 7–8.
Rows 7–16 form patt.
Cont in patt until approx 4yds (4m) of yarn A remains, ending after row 8.
Using A and B held together, rep rows 1–2 three times.
Bind (cast) off.

FINISHING
Do NOT press. Weave in yarn ends.

The ripple texture is easy to knit—you can see how short the written pattern is—and yet really effective.

wavy scarf

This traditional Shetland stitch pattern is really easy to knit and it has been given a contemporary twist by working it in chunky yarn. This version is really long, but you can knit it shorter and all in one color to tuck into the collar of your coat if you prefer.

Size
Approximately 12¼in (31cm) wide and 75in (190cm) long

Yarn suggestion
Three 3½ oz (100g) balls—approximately 450yds (411m)—of chunky-weight yarn, such as Sirdar Spree, in each of white (A) and blue (B)

Needles
Pair of US 10 (6.0mm) knitting needles

Other materials
Knitter's sewing needle

Gauge (tension)
20 stitches and 20 rows to 4in (10cm) over patt on US 10 (6.0mm) needles

Abbreviations
See page 101

Note that when changing yarn colors, you'll get neater edges, and avoid having to darn in dozens of yarn ends, if you change color away from the edge and carry the unused color up the work until needed again. On the first color-change row, knit the 3 edge sts using B, weaving in the color A yarn, then continue using B only. On the following color-change rows, carry the yarn loosely across the 3 edge sts, then knit in the strand with the new color.

One ball of yarn in each color is enough to knit a scarf that'll tuck neatly into your coat collar.

pattern

Using A, cast on 61 sts.
Rows 1, 2, and 3: Knit.
Row 4: K3, p to last 3 sts, k3.
Row 5 (RS): K4, * [yo, k1] twice, yo, [skpo] 3 times, k1, [k2tog] 3 times, [yo, k1] 3 times, rep from * two more times, k3.
Row 6: Knit.
Rows 3–6 form patt.
Cont in patt, work 4 rows B, 4 rows A until scarf measures 75in (190cm), ending with Row 6 in A.
Cont in A, k 1 row.
Bind (cast) off knitwise.

FINISHING
Weave in yarn ends.

lacy shawl

Vivid color updates a classic shape to create this pretty shawl. Wear it as a cover-up over a summer dress on cool evenings, as the perfect accessory to a party dress, or to add a great girly touch to jeans and a jacket. It's so flexible it'll never be left in the wardrobe. Knit the long gloves on page 60 to wear with it for a full burst of nostalgic style.

Size
Approximately 63in (160cm) along longest edge and approximately 25in (64cm) wide

Yarn suggestion
Eight ¾oz (25g) balls—approximately 1832yds (1680m)—of fine kid mohair yarn, such as Rowan Kidsilk Haze

Needles
Pair of US 6 (4.0mm) knitting needles

Other materials
Knitter's sewing needle

Gauge (tension)
24 stitches and 28 rows to 4in (10cm) square over st st using 2 strands of yarn held together and US 6 (4.0mm) needles

Abbreviations
See page 101

pattern

LACE PANEL

Worked over 15 sts.

Row 1: P1, yo, k1, yo, sk2po, k9, p1.
Row 2 and every foll alt row: K1, p13, k1.
Row 3: P1, [k1, yo] twice, k1, sk2po, k7, p1.
Row 5: P1, k2, yo, k1, yo, k2, sk2po, k5, p1.
Row 7: P1, k3, yo, k1, yo, k3, sk2po, k3, p1.
Row 9: P1, k9, k3tog, yo, k1, yo, p1.
Row 11: P1, k7, k3tog, [k1, yo] twice, k1, p1.
Row 13: P1, k5, k3tog, k2, yo, k1, yo, k2, p1.
Row 15: P1, k3, k3tog, k3, yo, k1, yo, k3, p1.
Row 16: As row 2.
These 16 rows form lace panel and are repeated.

SHAWL

Using 2 strands of yarn held together, cast on 21 sts.
Row 1: K5, p2, k13, inc purlwise in last st. *22 sts*
Row 2: Inc in first st, k1, p13, k2, p4, pick up loop lying between needles and place this loop onto right-hand needle (this loop does NOT count as a st), slip last st purlwise. *23 sts*
Row 3: K tog the slipped st and the picked-up loop, k4, p1, work next 15 sts as row 1 of lace panel, p1, k1.
Last 2 rows set position of lace panel and form slip st edging at straight (unshaped) row end edge.
Keeping patt correct as now set, cont as folls:
Row 4: Inc in first st, k1, patt to end. *24 sts*
Row 5: Patt 21 sts, p1, k2.
Row 6: Inc in first st, p1, k1, patt to end. *25 sts*
Row 7: Patt 21 sts, p1, k3.
Cont in this way, inc 1 st at beg of next and 4 foll alt rows, taking inc sts into st st. *30 sts*
Inc 1 st at end (shaped edge) of next row. *31 sts*
Inc 1 st at beg of next and foll 7 alt rows, taking inc sts into st st. *39 sts*
Row 33: Patt 6 sts, (work next 15 sts as lace panel) twice, p2, inc in last st. *40 sts*
**Inc 1 st at beg of next and foll 7 alt rows, taking inc sts into st st. *48 sts*
Inc 1 st at end (shaped edge) of next row. *49 sts*
Rep from ** ten more times, taking inc sts into st st until there are sufficient to work in lace panel patt. *139 sts*
Inc 1 st at beg of next row. *140 sts*
Work should now be 9 lace panels wide plus edge sts at straight edge, and row 16 of 13th rep of first lace panel should now have been completed.
***Work 1 row.
Keeping patt correct, dec 1 st at shaped edge of next and foll 6 alt rows, then on foll 2 rows. *131 sts*
Rep from *** twelve more times. *23 sts*
Row 16 of 26th rep of lace panel should now have been completed.
Bind (cast) off.

FRILL (MAKE 4)

Using 2 strands of yarn held together, cast on 226 sts very loosely.
Row 1: Knit.
Row 2: *K1, insert right needle point into st directly below next st on left needle and k this st, letting st above slip off left needle at same time, rep from * to last 2 sts, k2.
Rep row 2 until Frill measures 2½in (6cm).
Next row: *K2tog, rep from * to end. *113 sts*
Starting with a purl row, work in st st for 3 rows.
Bind (cast) off loosely.

FINISHING

Join ends of Frills to make one long strip, then sew bound (cast) off edge of Frills to shaped row end edge of Shawl.

Fabulous color makes this classic shawl a fashion-forward piece you'll love to wear.

giant cable scarf

A luxurious scarf (made here from pure Aran wool) that will be the envy of all your friends. The chunky cable makes it extra thick and warm, and with the super-long length you'll never be cold. You could also try this pattern with finer yarn for a skinnier and lighter-weight version of the scarf.

Size
Approximately 82½in (209.5cm) long and 8¼in (21cm) wide.

Yarn suggestion
Ten 3½oz (100g) balls—approximately 1859yds (1700m)—of worsted-weight yarn, such as Rowan Pure Wool Aran

Needles
Pair of US 11 (8.0mm) knitting needles

Other materials
Cable needle
Knitter's sewing needle

Gauge (tension)
18 stitches and 16 rows to 4in (10cm) square over patt using US 11 (8.0mm) needles and 2 strands of yarn held together

Abbreviations
C6F = slip next 3 sts onto cable needle and leave at front of work, k3, then k3 from cable needle.
C6B = slip next 3 sts onto cable needle and leave at back of work, k3, then k3 from cable needle.
See also page 101

pattern

SCARF
Using 2 strands of yarn held together, cast on 38 sts.
Row 1 (RS): Knit.
Row 2: Purl.
Row 3: K1, [C6F] six times, k1.
Row 4: Purl.
Row 5: Knit.
Row 6: Purl.
Row 7: K4, [C6B] five times, k4.
Row 8: Purl.
These 8 rows form patt.
Cont in patt until scarf measures approx 82½in (209.5cm), ending after patt row 4 or 8.
Bind (cast) off.

FINISHING
Do NOT press. Weave in yarn ends.
For fringe, cut 23½in (60cm) lengths of yarn.
Knot pairs of these lengths through every st along cast-on and bound-off (cast-off) edge.

beaded-rib scarf

This is a method of bead knitting that needs no special technique, all you have to do is slide the beads along the yarn—it's that easy. The beads help the scarf drape really well, as well as adding sparkle to make it a great accessory for day and night.

Size
Aproximately 4¼in (11cm) wide and 67in (170cm) long

Yarn suggestion
Three 1¾oz (50g) balls—approximately 327yds (300m)—of sport-weight yarn, such as Debbie Bliss Cathay

Needles
One US 3 (3.25mm) knitting needle
Pair of US 5 (3.75mm) knitting needles

Other materials
1,046 beads, approximately 3½oz (100g)
Sewing needle and thread
Knitter's sewing needle

Gauge (tension)
34 stitches and 24 rows to 4in (10cm) over plain rib using US 5 (3.75mm) needles

Abbreviations
B1 = slide a bead up the yarn so that it sits tight against the last stitch on the right-hand needle, the last stitch worked. See also page 101

Note: thread half of the beads onto one ball of yarn before starting to knit. Thread the other half onto another ball.
To thread beads onto the yarn, first tip them into a shallow dish. Thread a sewing needle with a short length of sewing thread and knot ends to make a loop. Slide the knot to one side and thread yarn end through loop. Pick up beads, three or four at a time, and slide them down the loop of thread and onto the yarn.

Take your yarn with you when you buy beads so you can check that the hole in the bead is large enough for the yarn to go through.

pattern

Start with a ball of yarn with approximately 200 beads threaded onto it.

Beaded cast on
Leaving a long end, make a slip knot on the single US 3 (3.25mm) needle.
Using the thumb cast on (see page 105), [B1, cast on 1 st] 33 times. *34 sts*
Change to US 5 (3.75mm) needles.
Row 1 (RS): K4, [p1, B1, p1, k2] to last 2 sts, k2.
Row 2: K2, [p2, k2] to end.
These 2 rows form beaded rib.
Work in beaded rib for 138 more rows.
Join in ball of yarn without beads.
Row 141: K4, [p2, k2] to last 2 sts, k2.
Row 142: K2, [p2, k2] to end.
These 2 rows form plain rib.
Work in plain rib for 151 more rows.
Join in second ball of yarn with beads.
Work 140 rows in beaded rib.
Bind (cast) off loosely in rib, bringing a bead up close between stitches each time.

FINISHING
Weave in yarn ends. Using a cloth to protect the beads, press according to yarn ball band.

join hands

armwarmers

Choose from a super-simple thumbless version of these armwarmers (the white ones), or the pattern with easy-to-work thumbs. Wear either style with three-quarter sleeves, pulled up for maximum warmth or pushed down for a casual look.

pattern (both alike)

Cast on 30 sts. Distribute these sts evenly over 3 of the double-pointed needles and place a round marker after the last st.
Using 4th needle, work in rounds as folls:
Round 1: *K1, p1, rep from * to end.
Rep round 1 seven more times.
Round 9: *K4, p1, rep from * to end.
Rep round 9 until work measures 15¼in (38cm).
Bind (cast) off.

For armwarmers with thumbs, work as given until armwarmer measures 12in (30cm), then as folls, keeping k4, p1 patt correct:

RIGHT ARMWARMER
Next round: Patt 15, slip next 6 sts onto a holder, patt 9 sts.
Next round: Patt 15, cast on 6 sts, patt 9 sts.
Work rounds in patt until work measures 15¼in (38cm).
Bind (cast) off.
Shape thumb
Rejoin yarn to cast on sts.
Pick up 6 sts across cast on sts, knit 6 sts from holder. *12 sts*
Distribute these sts evenly over 3 of the double-pointed needles.
Using 4th needle, work 8 rounds st st.
Bind (cast) off.

LEFT ARMWARMER
Next round: Patt 9, slip next 6 sts onto a holder, patt 15 sts.
Next round: Patt 9, cast on 6 sts, patt 15 sts.
Work rounds in patt until work measures 15¼in (38cm).
Bind (cast) off.
Shape thumb
Rejoin yarn to cast on sts.
Pick up 6 sts across cast on sts, knit 6 sts from holder. *12 sts*
Distribute these sts evenly over 3 of the double-pointed needles.
Using 4th needle, work 8 rounds st st.
Bind (cast) off.

FINISHING
Weave in yarn ends.

Size
One size

Yarn suggestion
Two 1¾oz (50g) balls—approximately 196yds (180m)—of worsted-weight yarn, such as Debbie Bliss Cashmerino Aran

Needles
Set of four double-pointed US 10 (6mm) knitting needles

Other materials
Round marker
Stitch holders

Gauge (tension)
18 stitches and 24 rows to 4in (10cm) square over patt (unstretched) using US 10 (6mm) needles

Abbreviations
See page 101

fair isle fingerless gloves

Designed to match the Fair Isle hat on page 18, these fingerless gloves are easier to make than they might look since, like the hat, they are knitted in the round. They use the same chart as the hat (see page 21).

Size
Approximately 8in (20cm) around hand

Yarn suggestion
Approximately 2¼oz (60g) of wool and wool-mix sport-weight yarn; 1½oz (40g) of this should be in the main color (A), and ¾oz (20g) in contrasting colors (B)

Needles
Set of four double-pointed US 6 (4mm) knitting needles
Set of four double-pointed US 3 (3.25mm) knitting needles

Other materials
Stitch holders
Knitter's sewing needle

Gauge (tension)
24 stitches and 26 rows to 4in (10cm) over Fair Isle patt using US 6 (4 mm) needles

Abbreviations
See page 101

Note: the gloves use the same chart as the hat (see page 21). This chart does not show any changes of color in the contrasting color (B). Change these B colors whenever you wish. Spread out the stitches on the right-hand needle each time you change color. This will stop the color rounds from pulling in.

pattern

LEFT GLOVE
Using US 3 (3.25mm) needles and A, cast on 48 sts.
Distribute these sts evenly over 3 of the double-pointed needles and place a round marker after the last st.
Using 4th needle, work in rounds as folls:
Round 1: [K2, p2] to end.
This round forms ribbing. Rib 11 more rounds.
Change to US 6 (4mm) needles.
Knit 1 round.
Work in patt from chart, as folls:
Round 1: Omit edge st, work 12 sts of first line of chart 4 times.
This round sets chart patt.
Cont in patt from chart changing colors for B whenever desired, work 21 more rounds from chart.
Thumb-opening round: Using A, k1, slip next 9 sts onto a holder and cast on in A 9 sts in their place, k38.
This round corresponds to 23rd line of chart.
Beg with 24th line of chart, patt 12 rounds from chart.
Cont in A.
K 2 rounds **.
1st finger: K first 3 sts of round and leave these 3 sts on a holder; using first dp needle, k next 6 st; using 2nd dp needle, k foll 6 sts; using 3rd dp needle, k next 3 sts, cast on 3 sts, leave remaining 30 sts on a holder. *18 sts*
Join in a round and k next 3 rounds from chart.
Bind (cast) off purlwise.
2nd finger: Slip 3 sts knitted at beg onto first dp needle, then pick up 3 sts from cast on sts of first finger; using 2nd needle, k next 6 sts from holder; using 3rd needle, cast on 3 sts; slip last 3 sts from holder onto spare needle and k these 3 sts. *18 sts*
Complete as first finger.
3rd finger: Using first needle, pick up 3 sts from cast on sts of 2nd finger; k next 3 sts from holder; using 2nd needle, k next 2 sts from holder; cast on 3 sts; slip last 5 sts from holder onto

spare needle; using 3rd needle, k these 5 sts. *16 sts*
Complete as first finger.

4th finger: Using first needle, pick up 3 sts from cast on sts of 3rd finger; k next 2 sts from holder; using 2nd needle, k foll 4 sts from holder; using 3rd needle, k last 5 sts from holder. *14 sts*
Complete as first finger.

Thumb: Using first needle, k9 from holder; using 2nd needle, pick up 1 st from row end and 4 sts from cast on sts; using 3rd needle, pick up 5 sts from cast on sts and 1 st from row end. *20 sts*
K 5 rounds from chart.
Bind (cast) off purlwise.

RIGHT GLOVE

Work as Left Glove to **.

4th finger: K first 18 sts of round and leave these 18 sts on a holder. Using first needle, k next 5 sts; using 2nd needle, k foll 4 sts; using 3rd needle, k next 2 sts; cast on 3 sts; leave 19 sts on second holder. *14 sts*
K 3 rounds.
Bind (cast) off purlwise.

3rd finger: Using first needle, pick up 3 sts from cast on sts of 4th finger; k2 sts from holder; using 2nd needle, k next 3 sts from holder; cast on 3 sts; slip last 5 sts from holder at beg onto spare needle; using 3rd needle, k these 5 sts. *16 sts*
Complete as 4th finger.

2nd finger: Slip 3 sts knitted at beg onto first needle; then pick up 3 sts from cast on sts of 2nd finger; using 2nd needle, k next 6 sts from holder; using 3rd needle, cast on 3 sts; slip last 3 sts from holder at beg onto spare needle and k these 3 sts. *18 sts*
Complete as 4th finger.

1st finger: Using first needle, k next 6 sts; using 2nd needle, k foll 6 sts; using 3rd needle, k last 3 sts; pick up 3 sts from cast on sts of 3rd finger. 18 sts.
Complete as 4th finger.

Right thumb: Work as for Left Thumb.

FINISHING

Weave in yarn ends. Press.

bobble wristwarmers

These cute wristwarmers have teeny bobbles that, when worked in a contrast color (like the ones in the photo), give them a spotty look, but in the same color will give an interesting textured feel. Wristwarmers don't restrict your hands at all, but do add coziness.

Size
Approximately 8in (20.5cm) around wrist and 5½in (14cm) long

Yarn suggestion
One 1¾oz (50g) ball—approximately 175yds (160m)—of 4-ply yarn, such as Rowan Cashsoft 4 ply, in each of taupe (A) and cream (B)

Needles
Set of four double-pointed US 3 (3.25mm) knitting needles

Other materials
Knitter's sewing needle

Gauge (tension)
30 stitches and 40 rows to 4in (10cm) square over patt using US 3 (3.25mm) needles.

Abbreviations
MB = make bobble using B as folls: [k1, yo, k1] all into next st, turn, p3, turn, k3, turn, p3, turn, sk2po.
Note: All bobbles are worked in B with all other sts worked in A. Strand B from bobble to bobble on WS of work, weaving it in every 2–3 sts.
See also page 101

pattern (both alike)

Using A, cast on 60 sts.
Distribute these sts evenly over 3 of the double-pointed needles and place a round marker after the last st.
Using 4th needle, work in rounds as folls:
Round 1 (RS): *K2, p2, rep from * to end.
Rep last round ten more times.
Rounds 12–13: Knit.
Round 14: *K1, MB, k4, rep from * to end.
Rounds 15–18: Knit.
Round 19: *K4, MB, k1, rep from * to end.
Rounds 20–21: Knit.
Rep rounds 12–21 twice more then rep rounds 12–16 once more.
Rep round 1 eleven times.
Bind (cast) off.

FINISHING
Do NOT press. Weave in yarn ends.

Knitting bobbles in the round might sound tricky, but it's not very hard to do and the look is worth the effort.

cabled mittens

Contemporary cable detailing makes these mittens a fashion statement, as well as being super-snug in winter weather. The cord is optional, but thread it through your coat sleeves and you'll never lose a mitten again.

Size
7½in (19cm) around hand

Yarn suggestion
Two 1¾oz (50g) balls—approximately 196yds (180m)—of heavy worsted yarn, such as Rowan All Seasons Cotton
One 1¾oz (50g) ball—approximately 196yds (180m)—of fingering-weight yarn, such as Rowan Cashsoft 4 ply

Needles
Set of 4 double-pointed US 9 (5.5mm) knitting needles
Two double-pointed US 2 (3.0mm) knitting needles or a French knitting bobbin

Other materials
Round marker
Cable needle
Stitch holders
Knitter's sewing needle

Gauge (tension)
16 stitches and 22 rows to 4in (10cm) square over st st using heavy worsted yarn and US 9 (5.5mm) needles

Abbreviations
C6B = slip next 3 sts onto cable needle and leave at back of work, k3, then k3 from cable needle
C6F = slip next 3 sts onto cable needle and leave at front of work, k3, then k3 from cable needle
See also page 101

pattern

RIGHT MITTEN
Using heavy-worsted yarn and US 9 (5.5mm) needles, cast on 28 sts.
Distribute these sts evenly over 3 of the double-pointed needles (10 sts on 2 needles, and 8 sts on 3rd needle) and place a round marker after the last st.
Using 4th needle, work in rounds as folls:
Round 1: *K2, p2, rep from * to end.
Rep this round seven more times.
Round 9: K5, inc in next st, k14, inc in next st, k3, inc in next st, k3. *31 sts*
Now work in cable patt as folls:
Rounds 10–12: Knit.
Round 13: K3, C6B, k to end.
Rounds 14–16: Knit.
Round 17: K6, C6F, k to end.
Rounds 10–17 form cable patt.
Work in patt for 15 more rounds.
Shape thumb
Slip first 15 sts and last 10 sts of last round onto a holder but do NOT break yarn.
**With RS facing, join in new ball of yarn to rem 6 sts and cont as folls:
Next round: Cast on and knit 6 sts, k6. *12 sts*
Distribute these 12 sts evenly over 3 needles (4 sts on each needle) and, using 4th needle, work in rounds as folls:
Next round: Knit.
Rep this round ten more times.
Next round: [Skpo, k2, k2tog] twice. *8 sts*
Next round: [Skpo, k2tog] twice. *4 sts*
Break yarn, thread through rem 4 sts. Pull up tight and fasten off.
Return to sts left on stitch holder before shaping thumb and, using yarn left with last round worked, cont as folls:
Round 33: Patt 15 sts, pick up and knit 6 sts from base of thumb, patt to end.
Distribute these 31 sts evenly over 3 needles and, using 4th needle, cont in cable patt as set as folls:
Work 17 rounds.**

A cord to thread through your sleeves means you'll never lose one of your fab cabled mittens.

Shape top

Round 51: K1, skpo, patt 9 sts, k2tog, k2, skpo, k10, k2tog, k1. *27 sts*

Round 52: K1, skpo, k7, k2tog, k2, skpo, k8, k2tog, k1. *23 sts*

Round 53: K1, skpo, k5, k2tog, k2, skpo, k6, k2tog, k1. *19 sts*

Round 54: K1, skpo, k3, k2tog, k2, skpo, k4, k2tog, k1. *15 sts*

Round 55: K1, skpo, k1, k2tog, k2, skpo, k2, k2tog, k1. *11 sts*

Round 56: K1, skpo, k3, skpo, k2tog, k1. *8 sts*

Break yarn and thread through rem 8 sts. Pull up tight and fasten off.

LEFT MITTEN

Using heavy-worsted yarn and US 9 (5.5mm) needles, cast on 28 sts.

Distribute these sts evenly over 3 of the double-pointed needles (10 sts on 2 needles, and 8 sts on 3rd needle) and place a round marker after the last st.

Using 4th needle, work in rounds as folls:

Round 1: *P2, k2, rep from * to end.

Rep this round seven more times.

Round 9: K6, inc in next st, k3, inc in next st, k7, inc in next st, k9. *31 sts*

Now work in cable patt as folls:

Rounds 10–12: Knit.

Round 13: K19, C6B, k to end.

Rounds 14–16: Knit.

Round 17: K22, C6F, k to end.

Rounds 10–17 form cable patt.

Work in patt for 15 more rounds.

Shape thumb

Slip first 10 sts and last 15 sts of last round onto a holder but do NOT break yarn.

Work as Right Mitten from ** to **.

Shape top

Round 51: K1, skpo, k10, k2tog, k2, skpo, patt 9 sts, k2tog, k1. *27 sts*

Round 52: K1, skpo, k8, k2tog, k2, skpo, k7, k2tog, k1. *23 sts*

Round 53: K1, skpo, k6, k2tog, k2, skpo, k5, k2tog, k1. *19 sts*

Round 54: K1, skpo, k4, k2tog, k2, skpo, k3, k2tog, k1. *15 sts*

Round 55: K1, skpo, k2, k2tog, k2, skpo, k1, k2tog, k1. *11 sts*

Round 56: K1, skpo, k2tog, k3, k2tog, k1. *8 sts*

Break yarn and thread through rem 8 sts. Pull up tight and fasten off.

CORD

Cast on 6 sts using fingering-weight yarn and US 2 (3.0mm) needles.

Row 1: K6, *without turning work slip these 6 sts to opposite end of needle and bring yarn to opposite end of work, pulling it quite tightly across WS of work, knit these 6 sts again, rep from * until cord is 63in (160cm) long.

Bind (cast) off.

Alternatively, use the fingering-weight yarn to make a length of French knitting to join the mittens.

FINISHING

Darn in yarn ends. Press carefully. Attach ends of cord to inside of cast on edge of each mitten at beginning of first round.

basketweave mitts

The mix of plain and textured squares create this lovely basketweave effect. The chunky yarn and longer length will keep your hands nice and warm, so make a different color pair to match every winter coat.

Size
Approximately 7¾in (20cm) around hand and 7¾in (20cm) long

Yarn suggestion
Two 3½oz (100g) balls—approximately 372yds (340m)—of worsted-weight yarn, such as Rowan Pure Wool Aran

Needles
Set of four double-pointed 4.5mm (US 7) knitting needles

Other materials
Knitter's sewing needle
Two stitch holders

Gauge (tension)
20 stitches and 28 rows to 4in (10cm) square over patt using US 7 (4.5mm) needles.

Abbreviations
See page 101

pattern

LEFT MITT
Cast on 40 sts.
Distribute these sts evenly over 3 of the double-pointed needles and place a round marker after the last st.
Using 4th needle, work in rounds as folls:
Round 1 (RS): *K2, p2, rep from * to end.
Rep last round six more times.
Rounds 8–9: Knit.
Round 10: *P2, k1, p2, k3, rep from * to end.
Round 11: *[P1, k1] twice, p1, k3, rep from * to end.
Rounds 12–13: As rounds 10–11.

Rounds 14–15: Knit.
Round 16: *P1, k3, p2, k1, p1, rep from * to end.
Round 17: *P1, k3, [p1, k1] twice, rep from * to end.
Rounds 18–19: As rounds 16–17.
Rounds 8–19 form patt.
Work in patt for a further 20 rounds, ending after patt round 15.
Shape thumb
Next row (RS): Patt 11 sts and slip these sts onto a holder, patt next 8 sts, turn and cast on 8 sts, turn, slip rem 21 sts of round onto 2nd holder.
Distribute 16 thumb sts evenly over over 3 of the double-pointed needles and place a round marker after the last st.
Using 4th needle, work work in patt as set in rounds for a further 10 rounds.
Bind (cast) off.
Slip 11 sts on first holder onto right needle, rejoin yarn and pick up and knit 8 sts from base of thumb, then patt rem 21 sts left on 2nd holder. *40 sts*
Cont in patt in rounds for a further 16 rounds, ending after patt round 8.
Bind (cast) off.

RIGHT MITT
Cast on 40 sts.
Distribute these sts evenly over 3 of the double-pointed needles and place a round marker after the last st.
Using 4th needle, work in rounds as folls:
Round 1 (RS): *P2, k2, rep from * to end.
Rep last round six more times.
Rounds 8–9: Knit.
Round 10: *K3, p2, k1, p2, rep from * to end.
Round 11: *K3, [p1, k1] twice, p1, rep from * to end.
Rounds 12–13: As rounds 10–11.
Rounds 14–15: Knit.
Round 16: *P1, k1, p2, k3, p1, rep from * to end.
Round 17: *[K1, p1] twice, k3, p1, rep from * to end.

Rounds 18–19: As rounds 16–17.

Rounds 8–19 form patt.

Work in patt for a further 20 rounds, ending after patt round 15.

Shape thumb

Next row (RS): Patt 21 sts and slip these sts onto a holder, patt next 8 sts, turn and cast on 8 sts, turn, slip rem 11 sts of round onto 2nd holder.

Distribute 16 thumb sts evenly over 3 needles and, using 4th needle, work in patt as set in rounds for a further 10 rounds. Bind (cast) off.

Slip 21 sts on first holder onto right needle, rejoin yarn and pick up and knit 8 sts from base of thumb, then patt rem 11 sts left on 2nd holder. *40 sts*

Cont in patt in rounds for a further 16 rounds, ending after patt round 8.

Bind (cast) off.

FINISHING

Do NOT press. Weave in yarn ends.

lacy long gloves

A pair of gorgeous gloves that coordinate with the lacy shawl on page 40. I've used cotton lace to trim them, which you could dye to match or contrast with your yarn if you wanted to.

Size
6¼in (16cm) around hand

Yarn suggestion
Two ¾oz (25g) balls—approximately 458yds (420m)—of fine kid mohair yarn, such as Rowan Kidsilk Haze

Needles
Set of four double-pointed US 6 (4.0mm) knitting needles

Other materials
Stitch holders
Round marker
Knitter's sewing needle
39in (1m) of ¾-in (2-cm) wide cotton lace
6 small buttons

Gauge (tension)
21 stitches and 22 rows to 4in (10cm) square over patt using 2 strands of yarn held together and US 6 (4.0mm) needles

Abbreviations
See page 101

pattern

RIGHT GLOVE
Using 2 strands of yarn held together and knitting needles, cast on 39 sts loosely.
Row 1: P1, *k1, p1, rep from * to end.
Row 2: K1, *p1, k1, rep from * to end.
These 2 rows form rib.
Work in rib for 2 rows more.
Row 5: Rib to last 3 sts, yo, k2tog (for first buttonhole), p1.
Work in rib for a further 2 rows.
Row 8: Rib 4, [work 2 tog, rib 5] five times. *34 sts*
Row 9: [P2, k9, k3tog, yo, k1, yo] twice, p1, yo, k2tog (for 2nd buttonhole), k1.
Row 10: P2, k2, [p13, k2] twice.
Row 11: *P2, k7, k3tog, [k1, yo] twice, k1, rep from * once more, p2, k2.
Row 12: As row 10.
Row 13: [P2, k5, k3tog, k2, yo, k1, yo, k2] twice, p1, yo, k2tog (for 3rd buttonhole), k1.
Row 14: As row 10.
Row 15: [P2, k3, k3tog, k3, yo, k1, yo, k3] twice, p2, k2.
Row 16: As row 10.
This completes cuff opening.
Now distribute the 34 sts evenly over 3 of the double-pointed needles and place a round marker after the last st.
Using 4th needle, work in rounds in lacy patt as folls:
Round 1: [P2, yo, k1, yo, sk2po, k9] twice, p2, k2.
Round 2 and every foll alt round: [P2, k13] twice, p2, k2.
Round 3: *P2, [k1, yo] twice, k1, sk2po, k7, rep from * once more, p2, k2.
Round 5: [P2, k2, yo, k1, yo, k2, sk2po, k5] twice, p2, k2.
Round 7: [P2, k3, yo, k1, yo, k3, sk2po, k3] twice, p2, k2.
Round 9: [P2, k9, k3tog, yo, k1, yo] twice, p2, k2.
Round 11: *P2, k7, k3tog, [k1, yo] twice, k1, rep from * once more, p2, k2.
Round 13: [P2, k5, k3tog, k2, yo, k1, yo, k2] twice, p2, k2.
Round 15: [P2, k3, k3tog, k3, yo, k1, yo, k3] twice, p2, k2.
Round 16: As round 2.
These 16 rounds form lacy patt.

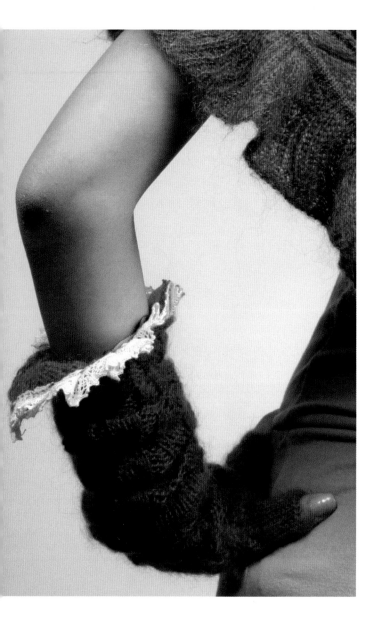

Work in lacy patt for a further 52 rounds.

Shape thumb

Slip first 7 sts and last 19 sts of last round onto a holder but do NOT break yarn.

With RS facing, join in new ball of yarn to rem 8 sts and cont as folls:

Next round: Cast on and knit 8 sts, k8. *16 sts*

Distribute the 16 sts evenly over 3 of the double-pointed needles (5 sts on 2 needles, and 6 on 3rd needle).

Using 4th needle, work in rounds as folls:

Next round: Knit.

Rep this round eight more times.

Bind (cast) off.

Return to sts left on holder before shaping thumb and, using yarn left with last round worked, cont as folls:

Next round: Patt 7 sts, pick up and knit 8 sts from base of thumb, patt to end. *34 sts*

Distribute the 34 sts evenly over 3 of the double-pointed needles.

Using 4th needle, cont in lacy patt for a further 13 rounds.

Bind (cast) off.

LEFT GLOVE

Using 2 strands of yarn held together and knitting needles, cast on 39 sts loosely.

Work in rib as given for Right Glove for 4 rows.

Row 5: P1, k1, yo, k2tog (for first buttonhole), rib to end.

Work in rib for a further 2 rows.

Row 8: Rib 4, [work 2 tog, rib 5] five times. *34 sts*

Row 9: K2, yo (for 2nd buttonhole), p2tog, [k9, k3tog, yo, k1, yo, p2] twice.

Row 10: K2, [k13, k2] twice, p2.

Row 11: K2, *p2, k7, k3tog, [k1, yo] twice, k1, rep from * once more, p2.

Row 12: As row 10.

Row 13: K2, yo, p2tog (for 3rd buttonhole), [k5, k3tog, k2, yo, k1, yo, k2, p2] twice.

Row 14: As row 10.

Row 15: K2, [p2, k3, k3tog, k3, yo, k1, yo, k3] twice, p2.

Row 16: As row 10.

This completes cuff opening.

Now distribute the 34 sts evenly over 3 of the double-pointed needles and place a round marker after the last st.

Using 4th needle, work in rounds in lacy patt as folls:

Round 1: K2, [p2, yo, k1, yo, sk2po, k9] twice, p2.

Round 2 and every foll alt round: K2, [p2, k13] twice, p2.

Round 3: K2, *p2, [k1, yo] twice, k1, sk2po, k7, rep from * once more, p2.

Round 5: K2, [p2, k2, yo, k1, yo, k2, sk2po, k5] twice, p2.

Round 7: K2, [p2, k3, yo, k1, yo, k3, sk2po, k3] twice, p2.

Round 9: K2, [p2, k9, k3tog, yo, k1, yo] twice, p2.

Round 11: K2, *p2, k7, k3tog, [k1, yo] twice, k1, rep from * once more, p2.

Round 13: K2, [p2, k5, k3tog, k2, yo, k1, yo, k2] twice, p2.

Round 15: K2, [p2, k3, k3tog, k3, yo, k1, yo, k3] twice, p2.

Round 16: As round 2.

These 16 rounds form lacy patt.

Work in lacy patt for a further 52 rounds.

Shape thumb

Slip first 19 sts and last 7 sts of last round onto a holder but do NOT break yarn.

With RS facing, join in new ball of yarn to rem 8 sts and cont as folls:

Next round: Cast on and knit 8 sts, k8. *16 sts*

Distribute the 16 sts evenly over 3 of the double-pointed needles (5 sts on 2 needles, and 6 on 3rd needle).

Using 4th needle, work in rounds as folls:

Next round: Knit.

Rep this round eight more times.

Bind (cast) off.

Return to sts left on holder before shaping thumb and, using yarn left with last round worked, cont as folls:

Next round: Patt 19 sts, pick up and knit 8 sts from base of thumb, patt to end.

Distribute these 34 sts evenly over 3 needles.

Using 4th needle, cont in lacy patt for a further 13 rounds.

Bind (cast) off.

FINISHING

Weave in yarn ends. Press according to yarn ball band. Attach buttons to correspond with buttonholes. Cut lace into two equal lengths and run gathering threads along straight edge. Using photograph as a guide and pulling up gathering threads to fit, sew lace in place around cuff opening and cast on edge.

Lace that's 100 percent cotton will dye beautifully, so if you can't find the color lace you want, create it yourself. Make sure the lace is pure cotton though, or the dye might not take very well.

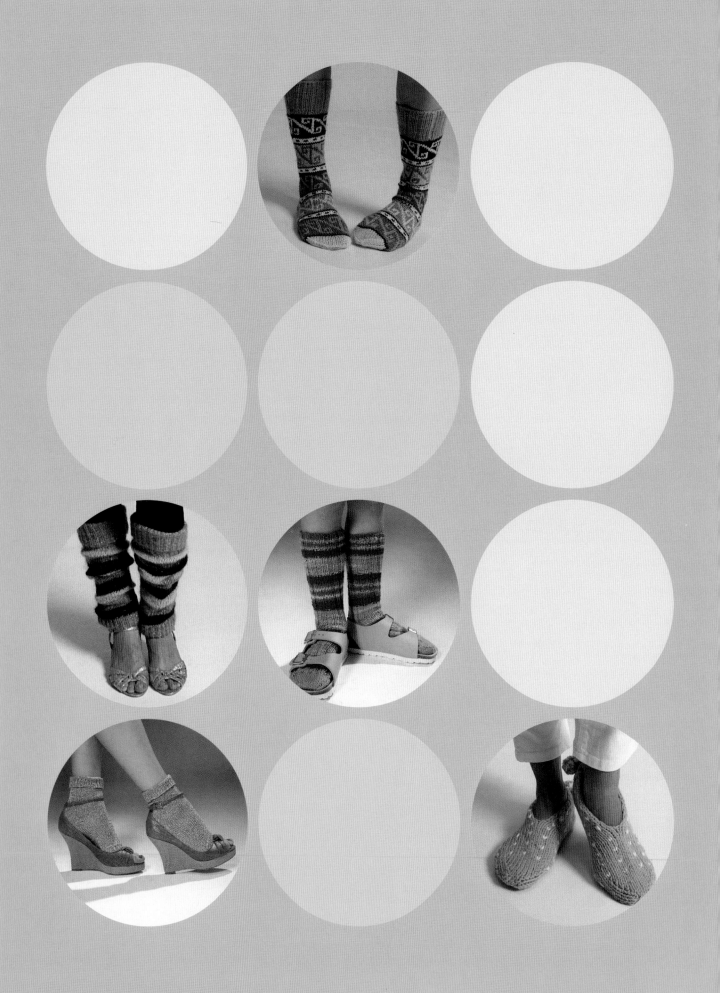

feet first

peep-toe socks

Knitted in glamorous gold, these little socks look fabulous with high heels— add bright nail polish for extra wow! Try knitting the socks in fine cotton yarn and wear them with flip-flops for summer style.

pattern (both alike)

Cast on 52 sts.
Distribute these sts evenly over 3 of the double-pointed needles and place a round marker after the last st.
Using 4th needle, work in rounds as folls:
Round 1: *K1, p1, rep from * to end.
Rep round 1 nine more times.
Round 11: Knit.
Rep round 11 until sock measures 4¾in (12cm), working k2tog at end of last round. *51 sts*
Cut yarn.
Shape heel
Slip next 13 sts on 1st needle, next 13 sts on 2nd needle, next 13 sts on 3rd needle and last 12 sts on end of 1st needle.
Rejoin yarn to beg of first needle.
Now working backward and forward in rows, not rounds, shape heel as folls:
Next row: K24, turn.
Next row: Sl 1, p23, turn.
Next row: Sl 1, k22, turn.
Next row: Sl 1, p21, turn.
Cont in this way, working one less st on every row until the foll rows have been worked:
Next row: Sl 1, p11, turn.
Next row: Sl 1, k11, turn.
Next row: Sl 1, p12, turn.
Cont in this way, working one more st on every row until the foll row has been worked:
Next row: Sl 1, p24, turn.
Slip next 17 sts on 1st needle, next 17 sts on 2nd needle and next 17 sts on 3rd needle. *51 sts*
Next round: Knit
Rep this last round until sock measures 5½in (14cm) from last dec row, decreasing one st at end of last round. *50 sts*
Next round: *K1, p1, rep from * to end.
Rep this last round nine more times.
Bind (cast) off in rib.

FINISHING
Weave in loose ends neatly.

Size
To fit shoe size US 6–9 (UK 3.5–6.5)

Yarn suggestion
Two ¾oz (25g) balls—approximately 118yds (200m)— of metallic crochet yarn, such as Anchor Artiste Metallic

Needles
Set of four double-pointed US 2 (3.0mm) knitting needles

Other materials
Round marker
Knitter's sewing needle

Gauge (tension)
42 rows and 30 stitches to 4in (10cm) square over st st using US 2 (3.0mm) needles

Abbreviations
See page 101

turkish socks

Based on a traditional Turkish design, these colorful, patterned socks work brilliantly with sandals, clogs, or boots. They also make great sofa socks for watching TV or bed socks if the weather gets really cold.

Size
Approx 9in (23cm) from toe to heel

Yarn suggestion
One 1¾oz (50g) ball—approximately 87yds (80m)—of worsted-weight yarn, such as Debbie Bliss Rialto Aran, in each of olive green (A), black (B), brick red (C), pistachio green (D), white (E), dull pale green (F), tan (G), red (H), jade green (J), pale blue (L), fuchsia pink (M), dark lilac (N), lemon (Q), and peach (R)

Needles
Set of four double-pointed US 7 (4.5mm) knitting needles

Other materials
Stitch holders
Knitter's sewing needle

Gauge (tension)
26 rows and 23 stitches to 4in (10cm) square over patt using US 7 (4.5mm) needles

Abbreviations
See page 101

pattern (both alike)

Using A, cast on 40 sts loosely.
Distribute these sts evenly over 3 of the double-pointed needles and place a round marker after the last st.
Using 4th needle, work in rounds as folls:
Rounds 1–21: *K3, p1tbl, rep from * to end.
Round 22: *K1, inc in next st, k1, p1tbl, rep from * to end. *50 sts*
Joining in and breaking off yarns as required and stranding yarn not in use loosely across WS of work, now work in patt from chart as folls:
Work all 18 rounds.
Using F instead of C and using G instead of D, work all 18 rounds again.
Using H instead of C and using J instead of D, work all 18 rounds again.
Shape heel
Next round: Using B k25, turn and using L cast on 25 sts. Break off B.
Slip rem 25 sts of main section onto a holder and distribute these 50 sts evenly over 3 of the double-pointed needles.
Using 4th needle and L, work in rounds as folls:
Next round: Using L, knit.
Rep last round twice more.
Join in M.
Next round: Using M k2, *using L k2, using M k2, rep from * to end.
Next round: Using L k1, *using M k2, using L k2, rep from * to last st, using M k1.
Next round: Using L k2, *using M k2, using L k2, rep from * to end.
Break off M and complete heel using L only.
Next round: [K1, skp, k19, k2tog, k1] twice. *46 sts*
**Next round: [K1, skp, k17, k2tog, k1] twice. *42 sts*
Next round: [K1, skp, k15, k2tog, k1] twice. *38 sts*
Next round: [K1, skp, k13, k2tog, k1] twice. *34 sts*
Next round: [K1, skp, k11, k2tog, k1] twice. *30 sts*
Next round: [K1, skp, k9, k2tog, k1] twice. *26 sts*
Next round: [K1, skp, k7, k2tog, k1] twice. *22 sts*
Next round: [K1, skp, k5, k2tog, k1] twice. *18 sts*

Next round: [K1, skp, k3, k2tog, k1] twice. *14 sts*
Next round: [K1, skp, k1, k2tog, k1] twice. *10 sts*
Next round: [K1, sk2po, k1] twice. *6 sts*
Break yarn and thread through rem 6 sts. Pull up tight and fasten off yarn securely.**

Shape foot
Return to sts of main section and, with RS facing and using B, pick up and knit 25 sts from cast-on edge of heel, k rem 25 sts of main section. *50 sts*
Distribute these sts evenly over 3 of the double-pointed needles and, using 4th needle, work in rounds as folls:
Starting with round 2 and using N instead of C and Q instead of D, work rounds 2 to 18 of chart.
Using G instead of C and J instead of D, work all 18 rounds of chart again.

Shape toe
Next round: Using B, [k1, skp, k19, k2tog, k1] twice. *46 sts*
Break off all contrasts, join in R.
Using R only, complete toe as for heel from ** to **.

FINISHING
Weave in yarn ends. Press according to yarn ball band.

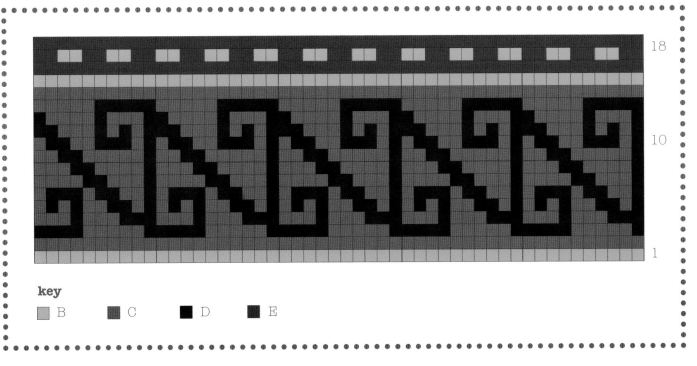

key

B   C   D   E

stirrup legwarmers

A fabulously retro 80s design, these easy-to-knit dancer's legwarmers look fantastic pulled halfway up your calf, or pushed right down around your ankles, whichever suits your leg shape best.

Size
Approx 10in (25.5cm) around calf

Yarn suggestion
Two 1¾oz (50g) balls—approximately 394yds (360m)—of fingering-weight yarn, such as Rowan Cashsoft 4 ply

Needles
Set of four double-pointed US 3 (3.25mm) knitting needles

Other materials
Knitter's sewing needle

Gauge (tension)
36 rows and 28 stitches to 4in (10cm) square over st st using US 3 (3.25mm) needles.

Abbreviations
See page 101

The true disco diva's fashion must-have, they're yours to knit.

pattern (both alike)

Cast on 72 sts.
Distribute these sts evenly over 3 of the double-pointed needles and place a round marker after the last st.
Using 4th needle, work in rounds as folls:
Round 1: *K1, p1, rep from * to end.
Rep the last round nine more times.
Next round: Knit.
This round forms st st, Cont in st st until until legwarmer measures 14½in (36cm) from cast on edge.
Shape stirrups
**Next row: K36, turn and work backward and forward in rows, not rounds, on these 36 sts.
Next row: Purl.
Cont in st st.
Next row: Bind (cast) off 4 sts, k to end.
Next row: Bind (cast) off 4 sts, p to end.
Next row: Bind (cast) off 3 sts, k to end.
Next row: Bind (cast) off 3 sts, p to end.
Next row: Bind (cast) off 2 sts, k to end.
Next row: Bind (cast) off 2 sts, p to end. *18 sts*
Next row: K1, skp, k to last 3 sts, k2tog, k1.
Next row: Purl.
Rep the last 2 rows five more times.
Work a further 12 rows in st st (1 row knit, 1 row purl).
Bind (cast) off. ******
With RS facing, rejoin yarn to rem sts. Work from ** to **.
Edgings (alike)
With RS facing, pick up and knit 50 sts from bound (cast) off edge to bound (cast) off edge.
Knit 3 rows.
Bind (cast) off.

FINISHING
Weave in yarn ends. Press according to yarn ball band. Join bound (cast) off edges and row ends.

spotty slippers

I've knitted these great slippers in girlie pink and white, but they look equally fab in almost any color combination. Make them to match your favorite PJs for toasty toes on winter mornings.

pattern

Using A, cast on 13 sts.
Distribute these sts evenly over 3 of the double-pointed needles.
Using 4th needle, work in rounds as folls:
Round 1: Knit.
Round 2: [K2, M1] twice, k5, [M1, k2] twice.
17 sts
Round 3: Knit.
Round 4: K3, M1, k2, M1, k7, M1, k2, M1, k3.
21 sts
Round 5: Knit.
Round 6: K4, M1, k2, M1, k9, M1, k2, M1, k4.
25 sts
Round 7: Knit.
Round 8: K5, M1, k2, M1, k11, M1, k2, M1, k5.
29 sts
Round 9: Knit.
Round 10: K6, M1, k2, M1, k13, M1, k2, M1, k6.
33 sts
Round 11: Knit.
Join in B.
Stranding yarn not in use loosely across WS of work, work in patt as folls:
Round 1: K2A, *k1B, k3A, rep from * to last 3 sts, k1B, k2A.
Rounds 2–4: Knit in A.
These 4 rounds form patt.
Work in patt for a further 12 rounds.
Now working backward and forward in rows, not rounds, cont as folls:
Next row: K2A, *k1B, k3A, rep from * to last 3 sts, k1B, k2A, turn.
Next row: Purl in A.
Next row: Knit in A.
Next row: Purl in A.
These 4 rows form patt for rest of slipper.
Work a further 14 rows, ending after a WS row.
Shape heel
Row 1: Patt 19 sts, sk2po, turn.
Row 2: Patt 6 sts, p3tog, turn.
Row 3: Patt 6 sts, sk2po, turn.
Rows 4–5: As rows 2–3.

Row 6: As row 2.
Row 7: Patt 6 sts, skp, turn.
Row 8: Patt 6 sts, p2tog, turn.
Rep last 2 rows six more times.
Bind (cast) off rem 7 sts.

FINISHING
Weave in yarn ends. Press according to yarn ball band. Join toe seam. Make four 1¼-in (3-cm) diameter pom-poms using A and B and sew two pom-poms to heel of each slipper.

Size
Approx 9in (23cm) from toe to heel
....

Yarn
One 3½oz (100g) ball—approximately 126 yds (115m)—of chunky-weight yarn, such as Rowan Cocoon in each of pink (A), and white (B)
....

Needles
Set of four double-pointed US 11 (8.0mm) knitting needles
....

Other materials
Knitter's sewing needle
....

Gauge (tension)
20 rows and 16 stitches to 4in (10cm) square over patt using US 11 (8.0mm) needles
....

Abbreviations
See page 101
....

2-button diamond socks

These ankle socks are so versatile: they look great with heels or flats, a frock or shorts, for a lunch date or an evening event. Make them in lots of colors to match everything you own.

Size
Approximately 8in (20cm) from heel to toe (unstretched)

Yarn suggestion
Two 1¾oz (50g) balls—approximately 274yds (250m)—of sport-weight yarn, such as Rowan Pure Wool DK

Needles
Pair of US 2 (3.0mm) knitting needles

Other materials
Stitch holders
Knitter's sewing needle
Four small buttons
Sewing needle and thread

Gauge (tension)
25 stitches and 35 rows to 4in (10cm) square over lace patt using US 2 (3.0mm) needles

Abbreviations
See page 101

Note: this is a small sock, but you can add in more pattern rows to extend it as necessary. After placing the 20 sts on the stitch holder, work in lace pattern until this knitted section is a bit shorter than the length of the top of your foot to where your toes start. Then shape the toe as per the pattern.

pattern

Lace patt
Row 1: K2, *yo, skpo, k5, k2tog, yo, k1, rep from * to last st, k1.
Row 2 and foll 6 alt rows: Purl.
Row 3: K3, *yo, skpo, k3, k2tog, yo, k3, rep from * to end.
Row 5: K4, *yo, skpo, k1, k2tog, yo, k5, rep from *, ending last rep, k4.
Row 7: K5, *yo, sk2po, yo, k7, rep from *, ending last rep, k5.
Row 9: K4, *k2tog, yo, k1, yo, skpo, k5, rep from *, ending last rep, k4.
Row 11: K3, *k2tog, yo, k3, yo, skpo, k3, rep from * to end.
Row 13: K2, *k2tog, yo, k5, yo, skpo, k1, rep from * to last st, k1.
Row 15: K1, k2tog, yo, k7,*yo, sk2po, yo, k7, rep from * to last 3 sts, yo, skpo, k1.
Row 16: Purl.
These 16 rows form lace patt and are repeated.

RIGHT SOCK

Cast on 49 sts.

Knit 2 rows.

Row 3 (RS): K2, yo, k2tog, k to end.

Knit 3 rows.

Row 7: As row 3.

Knit 3 rows.

Row 11: Bind (cast) off 6 sts, then work lace patt starting with row 1 (the stitch on the right-hand needle counts as the first knit stitch).

Cont until 40 rows of lace patt are completed.

Next row: Patt 23 sts, turn, place rem 20 sts on stitch holder.

Cont in patt until 75 rows of lace patt in total have been completed.

Knit 1 row.

Shape toe

Work in st st (1 row knit, 1 row purl), starting with a knit row.

Dec 1 st at each end of next and every alt row until 13 sts rem.

Work 1 row.

Bind (cast) off.

Shape heel

Rejoin yarn to 20 sts on stitch holder.

With right side facing, knit 1 row, inc 1 st at each end and 1 st in the center. *23 sts*

Work 11 rows st st without shaping.

**Next row: K14, k2tog, turn, *sl 1 purlwise, p5, p2tog, turn, sl 1 knitwise, k5, k2tog, turn, rep from * until 7 sts rem.

Next row: K7, pick up and knit 8 sts down heel.

Next row: P15, pick up and purl 8 sts down other side of heel.

Cont in st st until work measures same as top of sock to start of toe shaping.

Shape toe

Work in st st, starting with a knit row.

Dec 1 st at each end of next and every alt row until 13 sts rem.

Work 1 row.

Bind (cast) off.

LEFT SOCK

Cast on 49 sts.

Knit 1 row.

Row 2: K2, yo, k2tog, k to end.

Knit 3 rows.

Rep last 4 rows once more.

Row 10: Bind (cast) off 6 sts, k to end.

Work 40 rows of lace patt.

Next row: K20, patt 23 sts.

Next row: P23, turn, place rem 20 sts on stitch holder.

Cont in patt until 75 rows of lace patt in total have been completed.

Knit 1 row.

Shape toe

Work in st st, starting with a knit row.

Dec 1 st at each end of next and every alt row until 13 sts rem.

Work 1 row.

Bind (cast) off.

Shape heel

Rejoin yarn to 20 sts on stitch holder.

With wrong side facing, purl 1 row, inc 1 st at each end and 1 st in the center. *23 sts*

Work 10 rows st st without shaping.

Work as Right Sock from ** to complete.

FINISHING

Join foot and side seams neatly. Sew two buttons to garter stitch cuff to align with eyelet buttonholes.

argyle socks

Not just for keen golfers, these classic Argyle socks look super-cool with a knee-length wool skirt and chunky shoes, or peeping out of the tops of mid-calf leather boots.

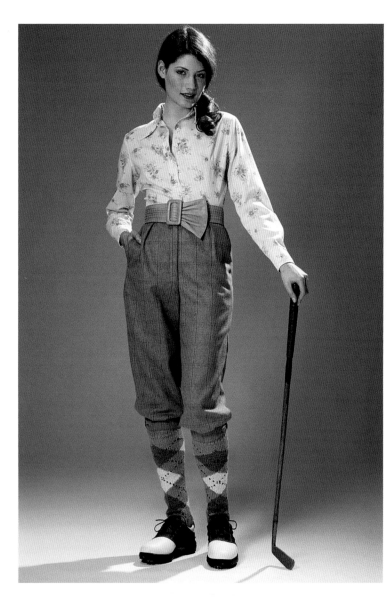

Size
Approx 9in (23cm) from toe to heel

Yarn
Three 1¾oz (50g) balls—approximately 327yds (300m)—of sport-weight yarn, such as Rowan Baby Alpaca, in fawn (A), and 1 ball—approximately 109yds (100m)—in each of cream (B), wine (C), and brown (D)

Needles
Pair of US 6 (4.0mm) knitting needles
Set of four double-pointed US 6 (4.0mm) knitting needles

Other materials
Knitter's sewing needle

Gauge (tension)
30 rows and 24 stitches to 4in (10cm) square over patt using US 6 (4.0mm) needles

Abbreviations
See page 101

pattern (both alike)

Using A, cast on 58 sts.
Row 1: *K1, p1, rep from * to end.
Rep the last row eleven more times.
Starting with a k row, work 8 rows st st.
Work 28 rows in patt from Chart. Rep Chart using C instead of B and B instead of C. Now work first 28 rows of Chart again.
Cont in A only.
Work a further 1¼in (3cm), ending with a p row and dec 7 sts evenly across row. *51 sts*
Cut yarn.
Change to double-pointed needles.

Shape heel

Slip next 13 sts on first needle, next 13 sts on second needle, next 13 sts on 3rd needle and last 12 sts on end of 1st needle.

Rejoin yarn to beg of first needle.

Next row: K24, turn.

Next row: Sl 1, p22, turn.

Next row: Sl 1, k21, turn.

Next row: Sl 1, p20, turn.

Cont in this way, working one less st on every row until the foll row has been worked:

Next row: Sl 1, p10, turn.

Next row: Sl 1, k11, turn.

Next row: Sl 1, p12, turn.

Cont in this way, working one more st on every row until the foll row has been worked:

Next row: Sl 1, p24, turn.

**Slip next 17 sts on first needle, next 17 sts on second needle and next 17 sts on 3rd needle.

Cont in rounds of st st until sock measures 5½in (14cm) from **, decreasing one st at end of last round.

Shape toe

Next round: [K1, skp, k19, K2tog, k1] twice.

Next round: K to end.

Next round: [K1, skp, k17, K2tog, k1] twice.

Next round: K to end.

Next round: [K1, skp, k15, K2tog, k1] twice.

Next round: K to end.

Cont in rounds decreasing on every alt round as set until the foll round has been worked.

Next round: [K1, skp, k7, K2tog, k1] twice.

Slip first 11 sts onto one needle and rem 11 sts onto a second needle.

Fold sock inside out and cast one st from each needle off together.

FINISHING

Weave in ends neatly, then press carefully. Join back leg seam.

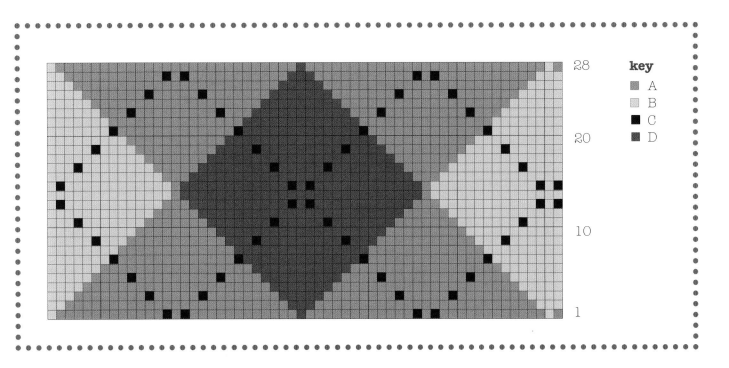

key
- ■ A
- ▨ B
- ■ C
- ■ D

sparkly legwarmers

Perfect with skinny jeans, you can combine these stripy sensations with strappy sandals or stiletto ankle boots to make your legs look extra long and slim.

Size
Approx 8¾in (22cm) around ankle and 10½in (27cm) around calf

Yarn suggestion
One ¾oz (25g) ball—approximately 229yds (210m)— of kid mohair yarn, such as Rowan Kidsilk Haze, in each of jade (A), camel (B), and black (C)
One spool of lurex sewing thread in each of silver and gold

Needles
Set of four double-pointed US 7 (4.5mm) knitting needles

Other materials
Knitter's sewing needle

Gauge (tension)
22 rows and 19 stitches to 4in (10cm) square over st st using US 7 (4.5mm) knitting needles

Note
Use 2 strands of mohair yarn AND lurex thread held together throughout. Use silver lurex thread with jade yarn and gold lurex thread with both camel and black yarn. Note that no reference is made to lurex thread in pattern.

pattern (both alike)

Using 2 strands of A, cast on 52 sts.
Distribute these sts evenly over 3 of the double-pointed needles and place a round marker after the last st.
Using 4th needle, work in rounds as folls:
Round 1: *K1, p1, rep from * to end.
Rep this round forty-nine more times.
Join in 2 strands of B.
Rounds 51–58: Knit in B.
Round 59: Using A, [k24, k2tog] twice. *50 sts*
Rounds 60–64: Knit in A.
Round 65: Using A, [k23, k2tog] twice. *48 sts*
Round 66: Knit in A.
Join in 2 strands of C.
Rounds 67–70: Knit in C.
Round 71: Using C, [k22, k2tog] twice. *46 sts*
Rounds 72–74: Knit in C.
Rounds 75–76: Knit in B.
Round 77: Using B, [k21, k2tog] twice. *44 sts*
Rounds 78–82: Knit in B.
Round 83: Using A, [k20, k2tog] twice. *42 sts*
Rounds 84–90: Knit in A.
Rounds 91–98: Knit in C.
Rounds 99–106: Knit in B.
Break off B.
Rounds 107–114: Knit in A.
Rounds 115–122: Knit in C.
Break off C and cont using A only.
Round 123: [K6, inc in next st] six times. *48 sts*
Rounds 124–133: As round 1.
Bind (cast) off in rib.

FINISHING
Weave in yarn ends. Press according to ball band.

lace-cuff boot socks

The deep cuffs of these socks are designed to fold over the tops of your boots and so prevent the socks sliding down inside. A subtle lace pattern and ribbon trim add a gorgeous girlie touch.

Size
Approx 9in (23cm) from toe to heel

Yarn suggestion
Three 1¾oz (50g) balls—approximately 534yds (495m)— of fingering-weight yarn, such as Garthenor 100% Organic Shetland

Needles
Set of four double-pointed US 3 (3.25mm) knitting needles

Other materials
Cable needle
Stitch holder
Knitter's sewing needle
40in (1m) of narrow ribbon
Four ⅝in (1.5cm) round beads

Gauge (tension)
36 rows and 28 stitches to 4in (10cm) square over st st using US 3 (3.25mm) needles

Abbreviations
Cr3R = slip next 2 sts onto cable needle and leave at front of work, p1, then p2 from cable needle
Cr3L = slip next st onto cable needle and leave at back of work, p2, then p1 from cable needle
See also page 101

pattern (both alike)

Cast on 104 sts. Distribute these sts evenly over 3 of the double-pointed needles and place a round marker after the last st. Using 4th needle, work in rounds as folls:

Round 1: *P2, sl 1, p3, sl 1, p1, rep from * to end.

Now work in patt as folls:

Round 2: *P2, sl 1, p3, sl 1, p1, rep from * to end.

Round 3: *Cr3R, p1, sl 1, p1, p1 enclosing loops of previous 2 rounds in st, p1, rep from * to end.

Round 4: *Sl 1, p3, rep from * to end.

Round 5: *Sl 1, p3, p1 enclosing loops of previous 2 rounds in st, p1, sl 1, p1, rep from * to end.

Round 6: *Cr3L, p3, sl 1, p1, rep from * to end.

Round 7: *P2, [sl 1, p1] twice, p1 enclosing loops of previous 2 rounds in st, p1, rep from * to end.

Round 8: *P2, sl 1, p1, sl 1, p3, rep from * to end.

Round 9: *Cr3R, p1, p1 enclosing loops of previous 2 rounds in st, p1, sl 1, p1, rep from * to end.

Round 10: *Sl 1, p5, sl 1, p1, rep from * to end.

Round 11: *Sl 1, p3, sl 1, p1, p1 enclosing loops of previous 2 rounds in st, p1, rep from * to end.

Round 12: *Cr3L, p1, sl 1, p3, rep from * to end.

Round 13: *P2, sl 1, p1, p1 enclosing loops of previous 2 rounds in st, p1, sl 1, p1, rep from * to end.

Rounds 2–13 form patt.

Cont in patt until sock measures 4in (10cm). Cuff completed.

Next round: [K12, k2tog, k12] four times. 100 sts

Next round: Knit.

Last round forms st st.

Work in st st for a further 8 rounds.

Place markers after first and last 25 sts—50 sts between markers.

Next round: *K to within 2 sts of marker, k2tog, slip marker onto right needle, k2togtbl, rep from * once more, k to end. *96 sts*

Work 9 rounds.

Rep last 10 rounds nine more times. *60 sts*

Work a further 9 rounds.

Shape heel

Now working backward and forward in rows, not rounds, shape heel as folls:

Row 1: K14, wrap next st, turn.
Row 2: P28, wrap next st, turn.
Row 3: K27, wrap next st, turn.
Row 4: P26, wrap next st, turn.
Row 5: K25, wrap next st, turn.
Row 6: P24, wrap next st, turn.
Row 7: K23, wrap next st, turn.
Row 8: P22, wrap next st, turn.
Row 9: K21, wrap next st, turn.
Row 10: P20, wrap next st, turn.
Row 11: K19, wrap next st, turn.
Row 12: P18, wrap next st, turn.
Row 13: K17, wrap next st, turn.
Row 14: P16, wrap next st, turn.
Row 15: K17, turn.
Row 16: P18, turn.
Row 17: K19, turn.
Row 18: P20, turn.
Row 19: K21, turn.
Row 20: P22, turn.
Row 21: K23, turn.
Row 22: P24, turn.
Row 23: K25, turn.
Row 24: P26, turn.
Row 25: K27, turn.
Row 26: P28, turn.
Row 27: K29, turn.
Row 28: P30.
Row 29: K15 but do NOT turn. Heel completed.

Now working in rounds again, distributing sts evenly over 3 needles, start to shape foot as folls:

Next round: Knit.

Rep last round until foot measures 7in (18cm) from back of heel.

Shape toe

Round 1: [K13, k2tog, k2togtbl, k13] twice. *56 sts*
Round 2 and foll 6 alt rounds: Knit.
Round 3: [K12, k2tog, k2togtbl, k12] twice. *52 sts*
Round 5: [K11, k2tog, k2togtbl, k11] twice. *48 sts*
Round 7: [K10, k2tog, k2togtbl, k10] twice. *44 sts*
Round 9: [K9, k2tog, k2togtbl, k9] twice. *40 sts*
Round 11: [K8, k2tog, k2togtbl, k8] twice. *36 sts*
Round 13: [K7, k2tog, k2togtbl, k7] twice. *32 sts*

Break yarn.

Slip first and last 8 sts onto one needle, and rem 16 sts onto another needle.

Graft together sts from both needles to close toe.

FINISHING

Weave in yarn ends. Press according to yarn ball band. Cut ribbon in half. Using photo as a guide and starting and ending at cast on edge, thread ribbon through sts of cuff in two parallel lines. Tie in a bow and thread beads onto ends of ribbon.

stripy socks

Ever-popular, you can knit these stripy socks in colors to match a child's favorite outfit; then plan on knitting lots more pairs to go with everything else they own.

Size
Approx 7in (18cm) from toe to heel

Yarn suggestion
One 1¾oz (50g) ball—approximately 230yds (210m)—of fingering-weight yarn, such as Regia 4 ply, in each of blue (A), beige (B), pink (C), and green (D)

Needles
Set of four double-pointed US 2 (3.0mm) knitting needles

Other materials
Stitch holder
Knitter's sewing needle

Gauge (tension)
42 rows and 30 stitches to 4in (10cm) square over st st using US 2 (3.0mm) needles

Abbreviations
See page 101

pattern (both socks)

Using A, cast on 44 sts.
Distribute these sts evenly over 3 of the double-pointed needles and place a round marker after the last st.
Using 4th needle, work in rounds as folls:
Left sock
Round 1: *P2, k2, rep from * to end.
Right sock
Round 1: *K2, p2, rep from * to end.
Both socks
This round forms rib.
Keeping rib correct and joining in colors as required, cont in stripes as folls:
Rounds 2–3: Using A.
Rounds 4–6: Using B.
Rounds 7–9: Using A.
Rounds 10–12: Using B.
Rounds 13–18: Using C.
Rounds 19–21: Using B.
Rounds 22–24: Using D.
Rounds 25–27: Using B.
Rounds 28–30: Using D.
Rounds 31–33: Using B.
Rounds 34–39: Using C.
Rounds 40–42: Using A.
Rounds 43–45: Using B.
Rounds 46–48: Using A.
Rounds 49–51: Using B.
Rounds 52–54: Using A.
Rounds 55–61: Using C.
Rounds 62–64: Using D.
Rounds 65–68: Using B.
Rounds 69–71: Using D.
Rounds 72–74: Using B.
Rounds 75–77: Using D.
Shape heel
Left sock
Slip first 22 sts onto holders.

You'll be kept busy knitting lots of these colorful socks—for your child and all of their friends.

Right sock

Slip last 22 sts onto holders.

Both socks

Rejoin C to rem 22 sts.

Working backward and forward in rows, not rounds, work on these 22 sts only for heel as folls:

Row 1: K21, wrap next st, turn.
Row 2: P20, wrap next st, turn.
Row 3: K19, wrap next st, turn.
Row 4: P18, wrap next st, turn.
Row 5: K17, wrap next st, turn.
Row 6: P16, wrap next st, turn.
Row 7: K15, wrap next st, turn.
Row 8: P14, wrap next st, turn.
Row 9: K13, wrap next st, turn.
Row 10: P12, wrap next st, turn.
Row 11: K11, wrap next st, turn.
Row 12: P10, wrap next st, turn.
Row 13: K11, turn.
Row 14: P12, turn.
Row 15: K13, turn.
Row 16: P14, turn.
Row 17: K15, turn.
Row 18: P16, turn.
Row 19: K17, turn.
Row 20: P18, turn.
Row 21: K19, turn.
Row 22: P20, turn.
Row 23: K21, turn.
Row 24: P22.

Break off C. Heel completed.

Distribute all 44 sts over 3 needles and, using 4th needle, work in rounds, starting at end of last complete round worked, as folls:

Left sock

Next round: Using B, rib 22, k22.

Right sock

Next round: Using B, k22, rib 22.

Both socks

Last round sets position of rib on top of foot and st st on sole.

Keeping sts correct as now set, cont in stripes as folls:

Using B, work 3 rounds.
Using A, work 5 rounds.
Using B, work 5 rounds.
Using C, work 4 rounds.
Using B, work 5 rounds.
Using D, work 5 rounds.
Using B, work 5 rounds.
Using A, work 4 rounds.
Using B, work 4 rounds.
Using C, work 4 rounds.
Using B, work 4 rounds.

Break off A, B and C and cont using D only.

Shape toe

Rounds 1–2: Knit.
Round 3: (K1, k2togtbl, k16, k2tog, k1) twice.
40 sts
Round 4: Knit.
Round 5: (K1, k2togtbl, k14, k2tog, k1) twice.
36 sts
Round 6: Knit.
Round 7: (K1, k2togtbl, k12, k2tog, k1) twice.
32 sts
Round 8: Knit.
Round 9: (K1, k2togtbl, k10, k2tog, k1) twice.
28 sts
Round 10: Knit.
Round 11: (K1, k2togtbl, k8, k2tog, k1) twice.
24 sts
Round 12: Knit.

Break yarn, leaving a long end. Slip first 12 sts onto one needle, and last 12 sts onto another needle. Using long end left at toe, graft together sts from both needles to close toe.

FINISHING

Weave in yarn ends. Press according to ball band.

other cool stuff

ribbed belt

Wear the widest version of this belt as a waist belt with a dress, or a narrower version with hipster jeans: either way it's fab. It's knitted here in gold, but other metallic colors will look amazing, too.

pattern

BUCKLE COVERING

Using a single end of yarn, cast on 6 sts.
Work in st st until the strip of knitted fabric, when slightly stretched, is long enough to wrap around the outside of the buckle.
Right-sides facing, fold strip in half lengthways, aligning cast on edge with sts on needle.
Knit first st on right-hand needle together with first st on cast on edge. Knit second st on right-hand needle together with second st on cast on edge. Pass first st on left-hand needle over second st. Cont in this way until all 6 sts are bound (cast) off.
Fasten off.
Slip loop of knitted fabric around buckle. Stitch row ends neatly together, twisting them so that the seam is on the inside of the buckle.

BELT

Using a single end of yarn, cast on 14(18:22) sts.
Work in st st until until work measures 2½in (6cm) from cast on, ending with a purl row.
Right side up, wrap knitted fabric around central bar of buckle. Knit first st on right-hand needle together with first st on cast on edge. Cont until all cast on sts have been knitted together with sts on needle.
Next row (WS): Purl.
Join in end of yarn from second ball.
Next row: *K2, p2, rep from * to last 2 sts, k2.
Next row: P2, k2, rep from * to last 2 sts, p2.
Rep these last 2 rows until work measures waist measurement plus 8in (20cm) (or desired length), ending with a WS row.
Shape end
1¼-in (3-cm) wide belt
**Next row: K2, p2, k2, p2tog, k2, p2, k2. *13 sts*
Next row: P2, k2, p2tog, k1, p2togtbl, k2, p2. *11 sts*
Next row: K2, p1, p2tog, p1, p2tog tbl, p1, k2. *9 sts*
Next row: P2, k2togtbl, k1, k2tog, p2. *7 sts*
Next row: K2, sl 1, p2tog, psso, k2. *5 sts*
Next row: P1, p3tog, P1. *3 sts*
Next row: Sk2po. *1 st*
Fasten off.**
1½-in (4-cm) wide belt
***Next row: K2, p2, k2, p1, p2tog twice, p1, k2, p2, k2. *16 sts*

Size
Approximately 1¼in/3cm (1½:2in/4:5cm) wide
To fit any waist measurement

Yarn suggestion
Two ¾oz (25g) balls—approximately 118yds (200m)—of lurex yarn, such as Anchor Artiste Metallic

Needles
Pair of US 2 (3.0mm) knitting needles

Other materials
Knitter's sewing needle
Buckle without tongue, to fit chosen belt width

Gauge (tension)
It is not necessary to achieve a specific gauge for this project

Abbreviations
See page 101

Next row: P2, k2, p2, k2togtbl, k2tog, p2, k2, p2. *14 sts*
Work from ** to ** of 1¼-in wide belt.
2-in (5-cm) wide belt
Next row: K2, p2, k2, p2, k1, k2togtbl, k2tog, k1, p2, k2, p2, k2. *20 sts*
Next row: P2, k2, p2, k2, p2tog twice, k2, p2, k2, p2. *18 sts*
Work as 1½-in wide belt from *** to end.

BELT LOOP
Using a single end of yarn, cast on 10 sts.
Work in st st until the knitted fabric measures twice the width of the belt, plus ¼in (0.5cm).
Bind (cast) off.

FINISHING
Wrong-sides facing, fold the belt loop in half lengthwise and sew row edges together. Sew cast on and bound (cast) off ends together, positioning row seam inside. Slip loop onto belt with seam at center back. Slide to approximately 4in (10cm) from the buckle and stitch in place at center back.

gold clutch bag

A glamorous twist on a knitted bag, this one is super-versatile. Here it's shown as a clutch with a wrist loop and a buckled closure. Add a 24in (60cm) strap to turn it into a shoulder bag that sits snugly under your arm, or a 43in (110cm) strap to wear it satchel-style.

Size
9½ x 6in (24 x 15cm)

Yarn suggestion
Four ¾oz (25g) balls—approximately 436yds (400m)—of lurex yarn, such as Anchor Artiste Metallic

Needles
Pair of US 2 (3.0mm) knitting needles
Set of four double-pointed US 2 (3.0mm) knitting needles

Other materials
Knitter's sewing needle

Gauge (tension)
32 stitches and 27 rows to 4in (10cm) square over 2 x 2 rib patt using 2 ends of yarn and US 2 (3.0mm) needles

Abbreviations
See page 101

pattern

BAG
Using 2 strands of yarn held together, cast on 78 sts.
Row 1 (RS): *K2, p2, rep from * to last 2 sts, k2.
Row 2: *P2, k2, rep from * to last 2 sts, p2.
Rep rows 1–2 until work measures 6in (15cm) from cast on edge, ending with a WS row.
First fold line
Next row: Knit.
Next row: Purl.

Next row: Knit.
Bag back
Next row: *P2, k2, rep from * eight times, p14, **k2, p2, rep from ** to end.
Next row: *K2, p2, rep from * eight times, k14, **p2, k2, rep from ** to end.
Rep last two rows until work measures 6in (15cm) from first fold line, ending with a RS row.
Second fold line
Next row: Purl.
Next row: Knit.
Next row: Purl.
Front flap
Next row: *K2, p2, rep from * eight times, k14, **p2, k2, rep from ** to end.
Next row: *P2, k2, rep from * eight times, p14, **k2, p2, rep from ** to end.
Rep last two rows six more times.
Next row: *K2, p2, rep from * eight times, k14, **p2, k2, rep from ** to end.
Shape corners
Keeping st st panel as set, work as folls:
Next row: P2, k2tog, work to last 4 sts, p2togtbl, k2.
Next row: K2, p2tog, work to last 4 sts, k2togtbl, p2.
Rep last two rows once more.
Bind (cast) off in patt.

LOOP
Using the double-pointed needles, work a 13in (33cm) cord (see page 57).

FINISHING
WS facing, fold bag at first fold line and sew up side seams.
Fold loop in half and sew to top of left-hand side seam.
If you want to make a closure for the bag, make a strap and buckle following the pattern for the ribbed belt (see page 90). Make the strap long enough to go around the bag and sew it to the center back of the bag.

string bag

Knit your own reusable grocery bag from ordinary parcel string; it's really easy and quick to do. The mesh will expand to hold lots and lots of stuff and you can keep an eye out for brightly colored string to make your version extra-special.

Size
Approximately 15¾in (40cm) wide and 14in (35.5cm) long

Yarn suggestion
Approximately 102yds (92m) of medium-weight jute string

Needles
US 19 (15.0mm) circular needle, 32in (81cm) long

Other materials
Size M/N or 13 (9.0mm) crochet hook (optional)

Gauge (tension)
6 stitches and 5½ rounds to 4in (10cm) over mesh patt, when stretched, using US 19 (15.0mm) circular needle

Abbreviations
See page 101

Note: to join in more string, knot the ends with a square knot (right over left and under, left over right and under) so it will be flat. Pull the knot tight, and trim the ends short.

pattern

Cast on 48 sts.
Place round marker after last st.
Round 1: [Yo, p2tog] to end.
This round forms mesh patt.
Work 16 more rounds.
Shape base
Dec round: [P2tog] to end. *24 sts*
P 1 round.
Work dec round again. *12 sts*
Leaving a very long end, cut the string.
Thread end of string twice around through stitches; then knot the end of the string between each stitch, thread end under knots, and trim off.

FINISHING
To make handles, thread string through cast-on edge of bag, then through again, about 5in (13cm) farther along, to make a doubled loop 14in (35.5cm) long as a base for first handle. Use crochet hook or your fingers to chain loops of string over this base to make a firm handle. Leaving a short end, cut string and thread end under handle loops to secure it. Make second handle opposite first handle.

The mesh pattern for this bag is just one row long, so anyone can knit it with ease.

tweed bag

A good-looking and capacious daily use bag that works equally well with casual jeans or a smart suit. There are many similar handles available in wood, metal, or plastic if you want to change the look, and you can add a fabric lining if you wish.

A tweed yarn looks good with wooden handles, but you might choose a smooth wool or cotton yarn to go with metal or plastic handles.

Size
Approximately 13 x 13in (33 x 33cm)

Yarn suggestion
Two 3½oz (100g) hanks—approximately 218yds (200m)—of chunky-weight yarn, such as Debbie Bliss Donegal Luxury Tweed Chunky

Needles
Pair of US 10½ (6.5mm) knitting needles

Other materials
Knitter's sewing needle
Two wooden handles

Gauge (tension)
12 stitches and 19 rows to 4in (10cm) square over st st using US 10½ (6.5mm) needles

Abbreviations
See page 101

pattern

BACK AND FRONT (both alike)
Cast on 42 sts.
Row 1: K2, *p2, k2, rep from * to end.
Row 2: P2, *k2, p2, rep from * to end.
Rep the last 2 rows three more times.**
Beg with a knit row, cont in st st.
Work 20 rows.
Rep from ** to ** once more.
Beg with a knit row cont in st st.
Work 8 rows.
Mark each end of last row with a contrast thread.
Dec row: K2, skpo, k to last 4 sts, k2tog, k2.
Next row: K2, p to the last 2 sts, k2.
Rep the last 2 rows five more times.
Rep from ** to ** once more.
Bind (cast) off.

HANDLE STRAPS (MAKE 4)
Cast on 6 sts.
Work 2 rows st st.
Bind (cast) off.

FINISHING
Join bottom and side seams as far as contrast threads. Thread handle straps through holes in handles and sew to top of bag.

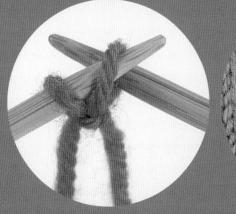

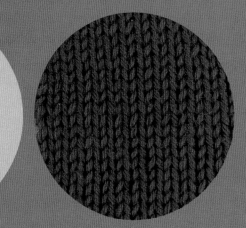

equipment and techniques

knitting equipment

You don't need much equipment to start knitting: here are some essentials and some useful pieces.

Knitting needles come in various sizes and materials; left to right, bamboo, metal, and plastic. Each pattern gives the size of needle you need, but the material is up to you. Novice knitters may find bamboo needles easiest to use since the yarn does not slip so easily on them, making dropping a stitch less likely.

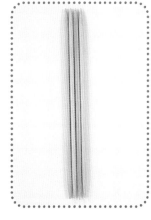

Double-pointed knitting needles have, as the name suggests, a point at each end. This allows you to knit from either end and so knit in the round. They, too, are available in different materials.

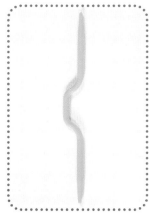

The cable needle shown is a cranked one, which holds the stitches securely while you work the cable, but you can also buy straight cable needles, which are quicker to use.

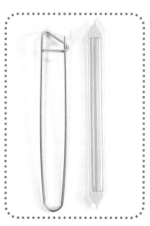

Stitch holders are used to keep some stitches safe while you work on another part of the project. They usually look like giant safety pins (left), but the double-ended type (right) are useful as you can knit straight off either end of them, rather than having to put the stitches back on a knitting needle first.

When you are working color knitting, wind lengths of the yarns you are using onto separate bobbins and knit from these to avoid ending up with a horrible tangle of balls of yarn.

Knitter's pins have blunt points to help prevent them splitting the yarn when you pin projects together before sewing up.

Point protectors are not essential, but they are useful. They stop the stitches falling off your needle when you are not knitting. They also stop the points of your knitting needles punching holes in your knitting bag.

A row counter is another non-essential item that you might find useful. Put it on a knitting needle and clock up each row as you work it, then you will never lose your place in a pattern.

Keep a pair of small, sharp scissors to hand for cutting yarn. Don't try and break yarn with your hands; some types are surprisingly strong.

There are various types of round marker, from metal rings to the pretty, beaded type shown. Alternatively, you can just use a loop of contrast yarn.

Knitter's sewing needles have a blunt point to help prevent them splitting the yarn when you are sewing up a project.

Use a solid ruler, made of either metal or plastic, to measure your gauge (tension) (see page 102).

needle sizes

Knitting needles are sold in standard sizes, though there are three different measuring systems.

US	metric	old UK and Canadian
50	25.0	–
35	19.0	–
19	15.0	–
15	10.0	000
13	9.0	00
11	8.0	0
11	7.5	1
10½	7.0	2
10½	6.5	3
10	6.0	4
9	5.5	5
8	5.0	6
7	4.5	7
6	4.0	8
5	3.75	9
4	3.5	–
3	3.25	10
2/3	3.0	11
2	2.75	12
1	2.25	13
0	2.0	14

abbreviations

Here is a list of the abbreviations you will find in the knitting patterns in this book.

A, B, C, etc	colors as indicated in the pattern	patt(s)	pattern(s)
alt	alternate	psso	pass slipped stitch over
approx	approximate	rem	remain, remaining
beg	begin, beginning, begins	rep(s)	repeat(s)
C4B	cable four (or number stated) back	rev st st	reverse stockinette (stocking) stitch
C4F	cable four (or number stated) forward	RS	right side
cont	continue	skpo	slip one, knit one, pass slipped stitch over
dec(s)	decrease, decreasing, decreases	sk2po	slip one, knit two together, pass slipped stitch over
DK	double knitting	sl	slip
foll(s)	following, follows	st(s)	stitch(es)
in	inch(es)	st st	stockinette (stocking) stitch
inc(s)	increase, increasing, increases	tbl	through the back loop
incl	including	tog	together
k2tog	knit two together	WS	wrong side
k	knit	yds	yards
M1	make one stitch	yo	yarn over
oz	ounce(s)	*	repeat instructions between/following * as instructed
p2tog	purl two together	[ ]	repeat instructions between [ ] as many times as instructed
p	purl		

gauge (tension)

When you buy a pattern it will specify the yarn you should use to knit it and the gauge (tension) the pattern requires. This is the number of stitches and rows to a specific measurement, usually 4in (10cm). It is important that you work to the gauge (tension) the pattern asks for or the finished item will be too big—if your gauge (tension) is too loose—or too small—if your gauge (tension) is too tight. So, even though you are desperate to start your project, take an hour or so to knit a swatch and measure it carefully.

knitting a gauge (tension) swatch

First, find the gauge (tension) information in the pattern. It will say something like: "22 stitches and 28 rows to 4in (10cm) square over st st using US 6 (4mm) needles." What this means is that, using the right sort of yarn and needles and working the right stitch pattern, in a piece of knitting measuring 4in by 4in (10cm by 10cm) you must have 22 stitches in one direction and 28 rows in the other direction.

So, use the yarn and needles specified in the pattern to cast on the number of stitches stated, plus ten. Knit the number of rows stated—in the stitch pattern specified—plus ten, then bind (cast) off. Make the bound (cast) off as loose as you can to avoid pulling in the top edge of the knitting.

altering your gauge (tension)

If you have the same numbers of stitches and rows as stated in the pattern, then you have the correct gauge (tension). You can now go ahead and knit the project your fingers have been itching to do.

However, if you do not have the right numbers of stitches and rows, you need to alter your gauge (tension). Do not do this by trying to knit more tightly or loosely. Everyone has a "natural" gauge (tension)—the gauge (tension) they naturally knit to—and if you try to knit to a different gauge (tension) your stitches will just be uneven. Also, you will usually forget that you are trying to knit more tightly and your natural gauge (tension) will reassert itself, then you are back to square one.

The way to alter your gauge (tension) is to change the size of the knitting needles you are using. If you have too few stitches and rows, knit the swatch again using needles one size smaller. So, if the pattern asks for US 8 (5mm) needles, try again using US 7 (4.5mm) needles. If you have too many stitches and rows, then try again with needles one size larger: US 9 (5.5mm) needles instead of US 8 (5mm).

This may sound time-consuming and annoying, but it's much better to knit a little square a few times than to spend more time and effort knitting a whole project that doesn't fit.

measuring your gauge (tension)

Now measure your gauge (tension). Do this carefully, or knitting the swatch will have been a waste of time. Measure a few stitches or rows in from the edges, as the cast on and bound (cast) off edges and row ends can be tighter or looser than the stitches in the middle of the knitting, which are those that matter.

Lay the swatch flat, without stretching it at all. To count the number of stitches, position a ruler so that 4in (10cm) is measured out a few stitches in from either edge. Put a knitter's pin into the swatch at either end of the measured distance. Count the number of stitches between the pins.

To count the number of rows, repeat the process, but lay the ruler vertically so that 4in (10cm) is measured out a few rows from either edge.

Measuring stitches.

Measuring rows.

knitting techniques

Practice any unfamiliar techniques on scrap yarn before embarking on your knitted project.

holding yarn and needles

There is no right or wrong way of holding the yarn and needles, so try these popular methods and use whichever feels most comfortable.

In the USA and UK the usual way is to hold the left-hand needle from above, like a knife, and the right-hand needle in the crook of your thumb, like a pen. The working yarn goes over the right index finger, under the second finger, and over the ring finger to control the gauge (tension). The right index finger moves back and forth to wind the yarn around the tip of the right-hand needle.

The other method, often called "continental method," also holds the right-hand needle like a pen, but the left-hand needle is held between the thumb and second finger. The working yarn goes over the left index finger, under the second and ring fingers, and over the little finger to control gauge (tension). The left index finger moves back and forth to wind the yarn around the tip of the needle.

The same principles apply when knitting in the round on four needles (see also page 110). Bring the lower end of the needle holding the stitches being worked over the top of the end of the needle below it to allow you to knit easily. You can ignore the two other needles holding stitches: as long as the stitches are not too close to either end of the needle, they won't fall off.

slip knot

The starting point for any piece of knitting is a slip knot. There is more than one way of making this, but the result is the same.

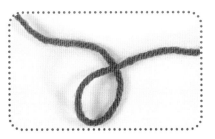

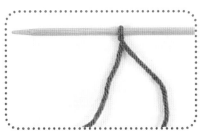

1 Lay the tail end of the yarn over the ball end to form a loop.

2 Bring the tail end under the loop of yarn. Slip the tip of a knitting needle under this tail end, as shown.

3 Pull on both ends of the yarn and the slip knot will tighten around the needle. This will be your first cast on stitch. After you have knitted the first couple of rows, you can pull gently on the tail end of the yarn to tighten the first stitch if it is a bit baggy.

cable cast on

This method of casting on produces a neat, firm edge that matches in perfectly with the look of stockinette (stocking) stitch (see page 109). Always make the slip knot about 6in (15cm) from the end of the yarn to leave enough to weave in the end later.

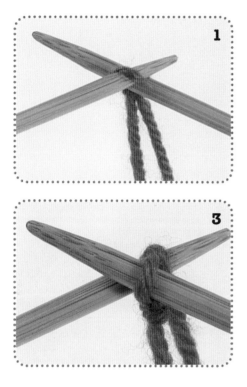

1 Hold the needle with the knot on in your left hand. From left to right, put the tip of the right-hand needle into the front of the knot.

2 *Wind the ball end of the yarn around the tip of the right-hand needle, going under and then over the top of the needle.

3 Bring the right-hand knitting needle, and the loop of yarn around the tip of it, through the slip knot.

4 Slip the loop of yarn on the right-hand needle onto the left-hand needle and pull gently on the ball end of the yarn to tighten the stitch. You have cast on a second stitch.

5 For all the following stitches, put the right-hand needle between the two previous stitches, instead of through the last stitch.

6 Repeat from * until you have cast on the number of stitches needed onto the needle.

thumb cast on

This cast on has an elastic edge that matches in well with the look of garter, rib, and seed (moss) stitch (see page 109). When casting on onto double-pointed needles, you can put a point protector on one end if you are worried about the stitches falling off. If you are working in double-knitting yarn, making a slip knot about 20in (50cm) from the end will allow you to cast on about 40 stitches.

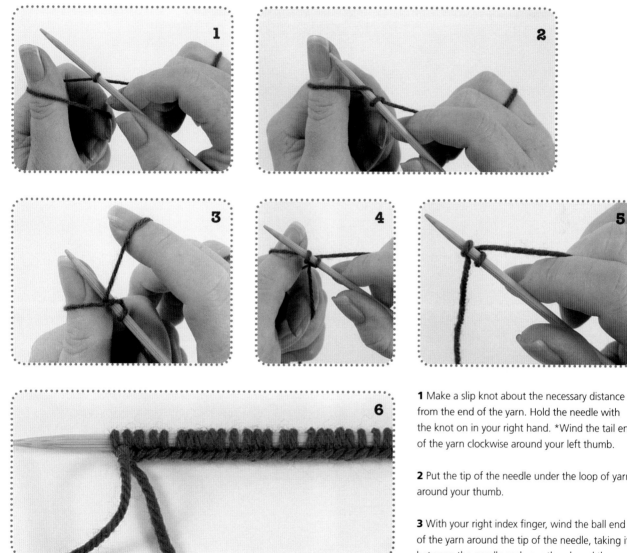

There are two popular styles of cast on and, unless the pattern says otherwise, you should choose the one that matches in best with the stitches you are knitting.

1 Make a slip knot about the necessary distance from the end of the yarn. Hold the needle with the knot on in your right hand. *Wind the tail end of the yarn clockwise around your left thumb.

2 Put the tip of the needle under the loop of yarn around your thumb.

3 With your right index finger, wind the ball end of the yarn around the tip of the needle, taking it between the needle and your thumb and then around to the front.

4 Bring the knitting needle, and the ball end loop around it, through the loop on your thumb.

5 Slip the loop off your thumb. Pull gently on the tail end of the yarn to tighten the stitch.

6 Repeat from * until you have cast on the number of stitches needed onto the needle.

knit stitch

This is the first and most basic stitch you need to learn to start knitting, and it is very similar to the cable cast on (see page 104). First, cast on the number of stitches needed for the project.

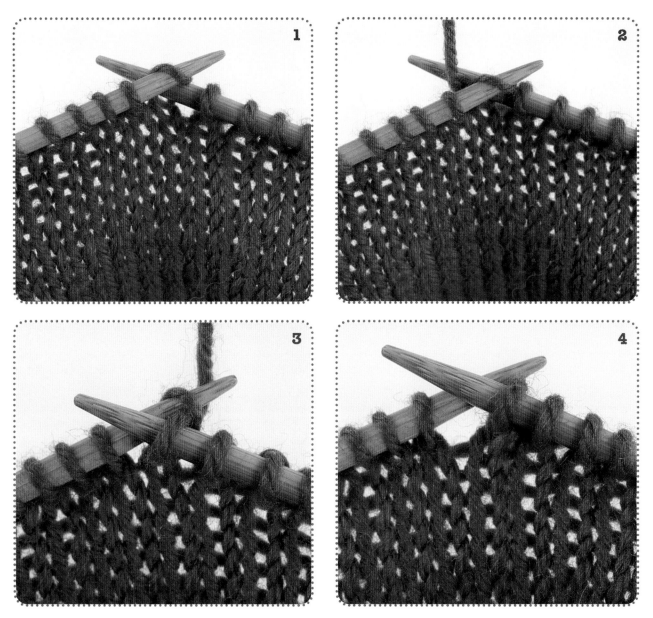

1 *From left to right, put the tip of the right-hand needle into the front of the next stitch on the left-hand needle.

2 Wind the working yarn around the tip of the right-hand needle, going under and then over the top of the needle.

3 Bring the right-hand needle, and the loop of yarn around it, through the stitch on the left-hand needle.

4 Keeping the loop on the right-hand needle, slip the original stitch off the left-hand needle. You have knitted a stitch. Repeat from * until you have knitted all the stitches on the left-hand needle. Then swap the needles in your hands and you are ready to begin the next row.

purl stitch

This is the other basic stitch used in knitting.

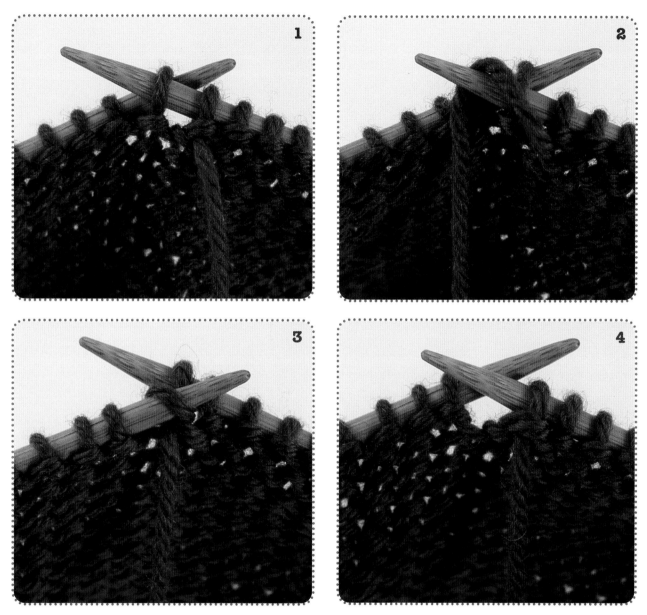

1 *From right to left, put the tip of the right-hand needle into the front of the next stitch on the left-hand needle.

2 From front to back, wind the working yarn over the tip of the right-hand needle.

3 Bring the right-hand needle, and the loop of yarn around it, through the stitch on the left-hand needle.

4 Keeping the loop on the right-hand needle, slip the original stitch off the left-hand needle. You have purled a stitch. Repeat from * until you have purled all the stitches on the left-hand needle. Then swap the needles in your hands and you are ready to begin the next row.

binding (casting) off

This is the way you finish off your knitting, securing the stitches so that they don't unravel. It is shown here on a knit row, but can be worked just as well on a purl row: simply purl the stitches instead of knitting them.

1 Knit the first two stitches on the left-hand needle.

2 *Put the tip of the left-hand needle into the first stitch you knitted and lift it over the second stitch. Drop this first stitch off both needles.

3 Knit another stitch and repeat from * to bind (cast) off all the stitches in turn.

4 When you have just one stitch left on the right-hand needle, pull gently to open it up a little and slip it off the needle. Cut the yarn 6in (15cm) from the knitting. Thread the cut end through the last stitch and pull gently on the cut end to tighten the stitch.

knitted fabrics

Now that you can knit, you can create knitted fabrics with different stitch patterns. Shown here are swatches of the four most popular simple knitted fabrics.

garter stitch

This is the most basic knitted fabric as it is made with knit stitches only.

To work garter stitch cast on as many stitches as you need. Knit every row.

stockinette (stocking) stitch (st st)

This is made by working alternate rows of knit and purl stitches. The other side is called reverse stockinette (stocking) stitch (rev st st).

To work st st, cast on as many stitches as you need.
Row 1: Knit.
Row 2: Purl.
Repeat rows 1–2. It's not really any more difficult than garter stitch. If you get confused as to whether you should be knitting or purling the next row, hold the needle with the stitches on in your left hand with the trailing yarn to the right. Look at the side facing you. If that is the right side, as shown above, then the next row will be a knit row. If the wrong side is facing you, the next row will be a purl row.

rib stitch

This is usually used to make cuffs and collars as it is very stretchy. There are various types of rib stitch: shown here is single rib (1 x 1 rib).

To work single rib stitch cast on an odd number of stitches.
Row 1: [K1, p1] rep to last st, k1.
Row 2: [P1, k1] rep to last st, p1.
Repeat rows 1–2.
After you have knitted the first stitch, bring the yarn between the tips of the needles to the front of the work ready to purl the next stitch. When you have purled, take the yarn to the back again to knit the next stitch.

seed (moss) stitch

This is a decorative stitch that makes a flat, firm border on garments and accessories.

To work seed (moss) stitch cast on an odd number of stitches.
Row 1: [K1, p1] rep to last st, k1.
Repeat row 1.
Bring the yarn forward to purl and take it back again to knit as for rib stitch. If you get confused as to which stitch you should be working next, look at the previous one. If it has a bump across it then it is a purl stitch and the next stitch will be knit. If the last stitch is smooth, then you knitted it and the next stitch will be purl.

knitting in the round

This is the technique used to work seamless tubes of knitting for making socks. It might seem fiddly at first, but do persevere as it isn't actually difficult once you get the hang of manipulating the four needles. An advantage of working in the round is that you only have to knit stitches—no purl rows—to make stockinette (stocking) stitch. You can more or less ignore the needles that you are not actually knitting with.

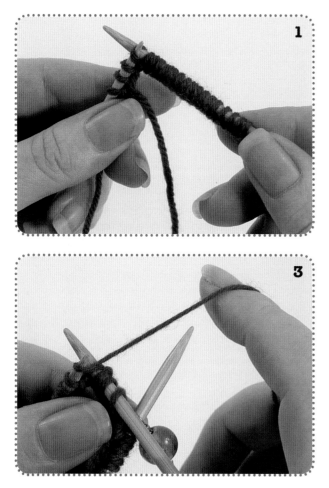

1 Cast on the correct number of stitches using the appropriate cast on method (see pages 104–105) and double-pointed needles. To distribute the stitches evenly between the needles, just slip one-third of them off one end of the needle onto a second needle. Slip another third of them off the other end of the needle onto a third needle. If you push the stitches to the middle of the needles they should just hang there without falling off.

2 Before you join the stitches into the round, slip a stitch marker onto the free end of one needle. Make sure that the row of stitches is lying in a straight line across the three needles and is not twisted at all. Now, put the fourth needle in the set through the first stitch you cast on. Wrap the working end of the yarn firmly around the tip of the fourth needle and knit the stitch, pulling it tight so that the three needles with stitches on form a triangle.

3 Continue knitting the stitches on the first needle. When they are all knitted, then that needle is freed up to become the spare needle for working the stitches on the next needle.

4 Just keep knitting the stitches off each needle in turn to create a knitted tube. When you reach the stitch marker, slip it onto the next needle so that you always know where the beginning of the round is. Knit the first stitch on each needle firmly, pulling the yarn tight, to prevent gaps appearing in the knitting where the needles "join." If they do appear, then occasionally knit one stitch off the next needle for a round to change the position of the "joins."

slipping stitches

A technique often used in lace knitting, slipped stitches can be worked knitwise or purlwise. If the pattern does not specify which way to slip a stitch, slip it knitwise on a knit row and purlwise on a purl row.

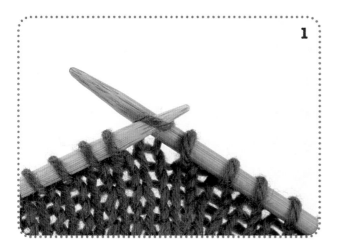

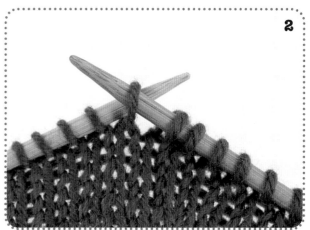

1 On a knit row, slip a stitch knitwise by putting the right-hand needle into the next stitch, as if to knit it, but slip it onto the needle without actually knitting it. Knit the next stitch in the usual way.

2 The principle is the same if you are slipping a stitch purlwise. Put the right-hand needle into the next stitch, as if to purl it, but slip it onto the needle without actually purling it. Knit the next stitch in the usual way.

pick up and knit

Use this technique to start knitting from a piece that has been bound (cast) off. It is one method of turning a sock heel (see also pages 114–115). The knitting pattern will tell you where and how many stitches to pick up.

1 Hold the yarn with which you are going to pick up the new stitches at the back of the finished piece. Put a knitting needle through the middle of the first stitch to be picked up from. At the back, loop the yarn over the tip of the needle.

2 Bring the needle back through the stitch, bringing the loop of yarn through with it. You have picked up one stitch.

increases

Increasing is making extra stitches in a row to make the knitting wider or to shape it. There are various different ways of doing this, but shown here are the most commonly used methods.

increase (inc)

This method involves knitting twice into a stitch. The increase is visible in the finished knitting as the second stitch made has a small bar of yarn across the bottom of it.

1 Knit to the position of the increase. Knit into the next stitch in the usual way (see page 106), but do not drop the original stitch off the left-hand needle.

2 Now knit into the back of the same stitch on the left-hand needle, then drop it off the needle. You have made two stitches out of one and so have increased by one stitch.

make one (M1)

This method involves creating a brand new stitch between two existing ones, It is almost completely invisible in the finished knitting.

1 Knit to the position of the increase. Using the tip of the left-hand needle, pick up the loop of yarn lying between the next two stitches. Pick it up by putting the tip of the needle through the front of the loop.

2 Knit into the back of the picked-up loop on the left-hand needle, then drop the loop. You have created a completely new stitch and so have increased by one stitch.

decreases

Decreasing involves taking away stitches in a row to make the knitting narrower. Again, here are the most popular methods. These decreases slant in different directions, so when used at either end of a row, they mirror each other.

knit two together (k2tog)

In this method you knit two stitches together to make one. The decrease slants to the right on a knit row.

Knit to the position of the decrease. From left to right, put the tip of the right-hand needle through the front of the second stitch from the end of the left-hand needle, then through the first one. Knit the two stitches together in the usual way, just as if they were one. You have made two stitches into one and so decreased by one stitch.

purl two together (p2tog)

This uses the same principle as k2tog to decrease stitches on a purl row. The decrease slants to the left on a purl row.

Purl to the position of the decrease. From right to left, put the tip of the right-hand needle through the next two stitches on the left-hand needle. Purl the two stitches together in the usual way, just as if they were one. You have made two stitches into one and so decreased by one stitch.

slip one, knit one pass slipped stitch over (skpo)

This method involves slipping a stitch and then passing the next one over it, rather like binding (casting) off. This decrease slants to the left on a knit row.

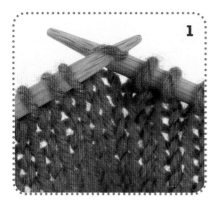

1 Knit to the position of the decrease. Put the right-hand needle into the next stitch, as if you were going to knit it, but slip it from the left-hand to the right-hand needle without knitting it.

2 Knit the next stitch on the left-hand needle in the usual way.

3 Put the tip of the left-hand needle into the slipped stitch and lift it over the knitted stitch, then drop it off both needles. You have made two stitches into one and so decreased by one stitch.

short-row shaping

This is a common method of turning the heel on a sock. Each row will tell you to knit a number of stitches, then "wrap next st, turn." Follow these wrapping techniques to wrap the next stitch in the row, then turn the knitting by swapping the needles in your hands.

on a knit row

Knit the number of stitches stated then wrap the next stitch as follows.

1 Slip the next stitch on the left-hand needle purlwise onto the right-hand needle (see page 111).

2 Bring the yarn forward between the tips of the needles.

3 Now slip the stitch back onto the left-hand needle, then take the yarn to the back again, thus wrapping it around the slipped stitch. Here, the yarn is shown as a loop so that you can see what is happening, but you must pull it taut. Now you are ready to turn the work and purl the next row.

picking up wraps on a knit row

Once the shaping rows are completed, you will knit across all the stitches in the row to start the foot section of the sock. When doing this it is essential to knit the wrap loops together with the slipped stitches they encircle to prevent holes forming. Follow the technique shown on each wrapped stitch as you get to it.

From the front and using the tip of the right-hand needle, pick up the wrap loop around the base of the slipped stitch. Slip this loop onto the tip of the left-hand needle and then knit the loop and stitch together as if they were one. The loop will not be visible on the right side of the work.

Short row shaping might look a bit complex, but practice the techniques on a swatch of knitting and you'll find that it isn't tricky to master.

on a purl row

Purl the number of stitches stated then wrap the next stitch as follows.

1 Slip the next stitch on the left-hand needle purlwise onto the right-hand needle (see page 111).

2 Take the yarn back between the tips of the needles.

3 Now slip the stitch back onto the left-hand needle, then bring the yarn to the front between the needles again, thus wrapping it around the slipped stitch. Now you are ready to turn the work and knit the next row.

picking up wraps on a purl row

Working across the knitting in the opposite direction to a knit row, follow the technique shown on each wrapped stitch as you get to it.

From behind and using the tip of the right-hand needle, pick up the wrap loop around the base of the slipped stitch. Slip this loop onto the tip of the left-hand needle and then purl the loop and stitch together as if they were one. The loop will not be visible on the right side of the work.

cables

Cabling is a technique that looks difficult, but is in fact easy. All you are doing is swapping the positions on the needle of groups of stitches. Shown here is cable four, but you can cable two, four, or six stitches just as easily. Cables are usually worked in stockinette (stocking) stitch with a background of reverse stockinette (stocking) stitch, as shown.

cable four back (C4B)

A back cable twists to the right on the right side of the work.

1 Purl to the position of the cable. Take the yarn between the tips of the needles to the back of the work.

2 Slip the next two stitches on the left-hand needle onto a cable needle.

3 With the cable needle at the back of the work, knit the next two stitches on the left-hand needle. Just ignore the cable needle while doing this.

4 Now knit the two stitches on the cable needle. Just slide them to the end of the needle and knit them in the usual way. Purl to the end of the row, or to the next cable.

cable four front (C4F)

A front (or "forward," as it is also known) cable twists to the left on the right side of the work. Work it in a similar way to a front cable, but leave the cable needle at the front of the work instead of at the back while you knit the next two stitches on the left-hand needle.

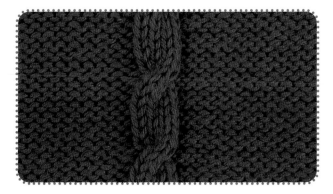

This swatch of C4B is worked over eight rows; that is to say, the cable is twisted on every eighth row of knitting.

crosses

Crossed stitches use the same principle as cables, but are subtler and often used in lace patterns. Here, the technique is shown on reverse stockinette (stocking) stitch: to work it on stockinette (stocking) stitch, knit the stitches instead of purling them.

cross three right (cr3R)

The stitches cross to the right on the right side of the work.

1 Purl to the position of the cross. Slip the next two stitches on the left-hand needle onto a cable needle and leave this at the front of the work.

2 Purl the next stitch on the left-hand needle.

3 Then purl the two stitches from the cable needle. Purl to the next stitch instruction.

cross three left (cr3L)

The stitches cross to the left on the right side of the work. Work this in a similar way to cr3R, but slip just one stitch onto the cable needle and leave it at the back of the work. Purl two stitches from the left-hand needle, then purl the stitch from the cable needle.

bobbles

Bobbles can be big and chunky or small and sweet and there are various different ways to produce them; shown here is the technique used in this book.

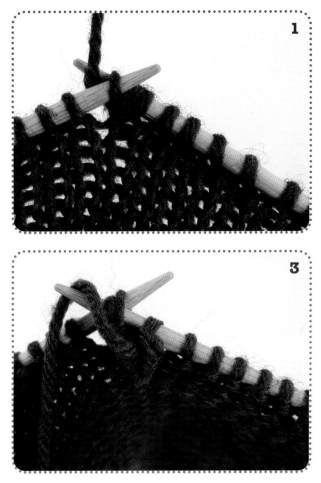

1 Knit to the position of the bobble. Knit into the front and back of the next stitch in the same way as for inc (see page 112), but do this twice so that you have made four stitches out of one.

2 Turn the work by swapping the needles in your hands. Purl the four stitches created in Step 1. Turn the work again and knit the four stitches.

3 Turn the work again. Work p2tog (see page 113) twice to reduce the four stitches to two.

4 Turn the work for the last time and work k2tog (see page 113) to reduce the two stitches to one and thus complete the bobble and return to the original stitch count on the row.

When you have completed the knitting you can tweak and shape the bobbles a little with your fingers if necessary.

yarnover (yo)

These are the staple ingredient of lace knitting. A yarnover produces a small eyelet that when arranged with others in a pattern produces the lace effect. Eyelets worked in this way are also used to make buttonholes for small buttons. Working k2tog (see page 113) after a yarnover reduces the number of stitches back to the original stitch count.

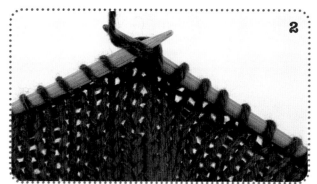

1 On a knit row, knit to the position of the eyelet. Bring the yarn forward between the tips of the knitting needles: this is known as "yarnover" (yo).

2 Take the yarn over the top of the right-hand needle and to the back, ready to knit the next two stitches on the left-hand needle together (k2tog). When you are purling back across the stitches, purl the yarnover as if it were a normal stitch.

through the back loop (tbl)

Knitting or purling a stitch through the back of the loop (rather than through the front as normal), twists the stitch. The effect is subtle and is used mainly as either an element in lace knitting, or in shaping: for example, "k2togtbl" means knit two together (see page 113), but through the back loops.

To knit a stitch through the back loop, put the right-hand needle from right to left through the stitch, but putting it behind the left-hand needle. Take the yarn around the tip of the right-hand needle in the usual way and knit the stitch.

To purl a stitch through the back loop, put the right-hand needle from left to right through the back of the stitch: when you straighten the left-hand needle the stitch will be twisted around it, as shown. Take the yarn around the tip of the right-hand needle in the usual way and purl the stitch.

color knitting

There are two main techniques for color knitting: Fair Isle and intarsia. For both techniques it is important to twist the yarns around one another as shown to prevent holes appearing between the different-colored yarns. Whether colors change in straight lines or on the diagonal will, of course, depend on the motif you are knitting. Shown here are the principles of making all the color changes.

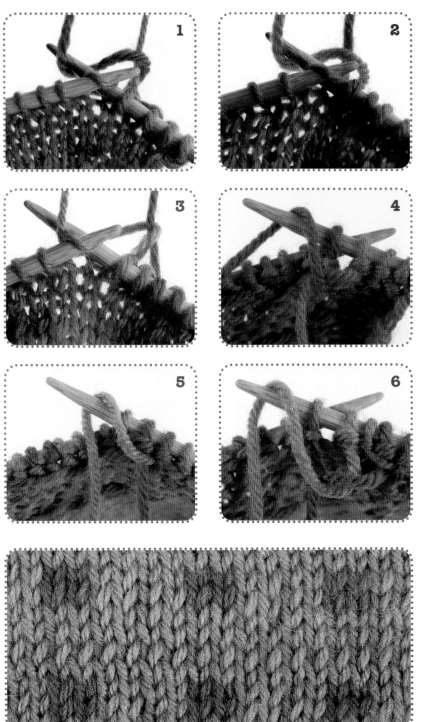

fair isle

This method strands yarn across the back of the work and is used to knit continuous patterns and motifs in the round. Do not pull the yarn tight across the back of the work or it will pucker up. However, stranding it too loosely will result in loops on the back. Practice to get the balance right.

1 On a knit row, knit to the first color change. Bring the new color yarn (purple) from under the original color yarn (pink) and then around the needle to knit the stitch.

2 Knit the stitches in the new yarn. When you get to the next color change, bring that yarn (pink) from under the new yarn (purple) and around the needle to knit the stitch.

3 If the interval between color changes is more than three stitches, you will need to weave the yarn not in use into the back of a stitch to prevent long loops forming. Bring the working yarn under the yarn not in use, then knit the next stitch in the working yarn. Here the purple yarn is being woven into the back of a pink stitch.

4 On a purl row, purl to the first color change. Bring the new color yarn (purple) under the original color (pink) and then around the needle to purl the stitch.

5 At the next color change, bring the original yarn (here it is pink) over the new yarn (purple) and purl the stitches.

6 If the interval between color changes is more than three stitches you must also weave in the yarn not in use on purl rows.

Yarn woven into the back of a stitch may show a little on the front, either as a slight pucker or as a spot of color between stitches.

intarsia

This method uses a separate ball of yarn for each colored area. To avoid tangling the yarns, wind long lengths onto bobbins and knit from these.

1 On a knit row, knit to the first color change. Bring the new color yarn (magenta) over the original color yarn (blue) and then around the needle to knit the stitch.

2 Knit the stitches in the new color yarn. When you get to the next color change, bring that yarn (magenta) over the original color yarn (blue) and around the needle to knit the stitch. To knit the next stitch on the row shown, bring the blue yarn over the magenta yarn: this is shown in Step 4 on a purl row where it can be seen more easily.

3 On a purl row, purl to the first color change. Bring the new color yarn (magenta) under the original color yarn (blue) and then around the needle to purl the stitch.

4 To purl the next stitch in the new color yarn, bring that yarn (magenta) under the original color yarn (blue) and around the needle to knit the stitch.

5 To work the next color change, bring the new color (now blue) over the old color (magenta) on both knit and purl rows.

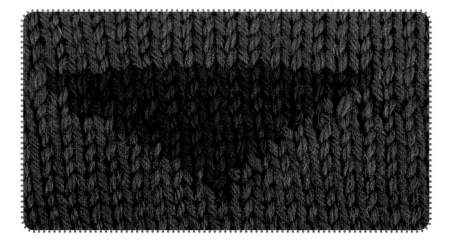

Weaving in ends neatly (see page 122) gives you the opportunity to tighten up any loose stitches at the beginning and end of an intarsia color motif.

using a stitch holder

Some patterns tell you to place a certain number of stitches on a holder. You will work the remaining stitches on the knitting needles, then come back to the stitches on the holder and work those.

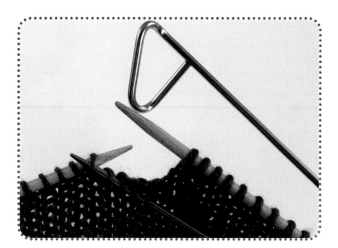

Simply slip the required number of stitches from the needle onto the holder. Make sure that the holder is securely closed, then ignore it until the pattern tells you otherwise. At that point, slip the stitches back onto the needle and work them as instructed.

joining in new yarn

When you reach the end of a ball of yarn you need to join in a new one to continue knitting. You also use this method to join in a different-colored yarn in color knitting (see pages 120–121).

If you are joining in new yarn because you have come to the end of a ball, join it in at the end of a row. You must have a length of yarn approximately four times the width of the knitting to knit one row. Tie the new yarn in a loose single knot around the tail end of the old yarn. Slide the knot up to the work and pull it tight. Leave a 6in (15cm) tail on each yarn to weave in later.

weaving in ends

When you have finished your knitting, you need to weave in any ends from casting on, binding (casting) off, and joining new yarn.

Thread a knitter's sewing needle with the tail of yarn. Take the needle back and forth, not up and over, through the backs of several stitches. Go through approximately four stitches in one direction, then work back through the last two again. If you are weaving in ends from color knitting, weave the tails into stitches of the same color to stop them showing on the front.

blocking

Once you have finished your knitting project, it will benefit from being blocked. This smooths out the fabric, helps hide any small imperfections, and makes the project much easier to sew up.

On an ironing board, lay out your project pieces without stretching them. Measure each piece and ease them to the correct size and shape. Pin the pieces to the board by pushing dressmaker's pins through the edge stitches into the board.

Carefully following the instructions on the yarn ball band, press all the pieces. Leave them pinned out until they are completely cold. Then take out all the pins and you are ready to start sewing up your project.

sewing up

Many people rush this stage of making a knitting project, which is a mistake. Take your time and your seams will be smooth and neat, giving your knitting a professional finish. Use the yarn you used to knit the project to sew it up, though if the yarn is very fine or breaks easily, use a stronger one in the same fiber and color.

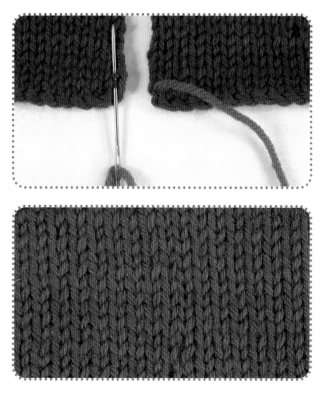

1 Thread a knitter's sewing needle with a long length of yarn. Here, a contrast color has been used for clarity. Secure the yarn on the back of one of the pieces to be joined by taking it over a couple of stitches, a couple of times. Bring the needle to the front of the fabric, bringing it up between the first two stitches on the first row.

2 Right-side up, lay the other project piece to be joined next to the first piece. From the front, take the needle through the fabric between the first two stitches on the first row and up under the bars of two stitches. Pull the yarn through.

3 Take the needle back through where it came out on the first piece and under the bars of two stitches. Take it back to the other piece, through where it came out and up under the bars of two stitches. Zigzag between the pieces, taking the needle under two stitch bars each time. Gently pull the yarn to close the seam as you work.

Worked neatly, a mattress stitched seam blends into the knitted fabric.

swiss darning

Also known as duplicate stitch, this is a way of adding different-colored stitches to a piece of stockinette (stocking) stitch knitting once it is finished. Always work Swiss darning using a yarn that is the same weight as the yarn the fabric is knitted in or it won't look very neat.

a vertical row

Use this method to work vertical rows of colored stitches.

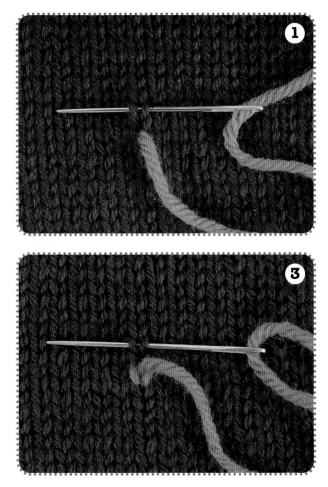

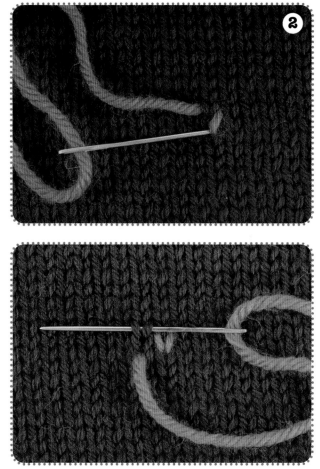

1 Thread a knitter's sewing needle with a long length of yarn. From the back, bring the needle up through the knitted fabric at the base of a stitch. *Take the needle under the two loops of the stitch above, as shown.

2 Gently pull the yarn through, then take the needle back down through the base of the stitch, where it came out.

3 Bring the yarn up through the knitted fabric at the base of the next stitch up. Repeat from * until the row is stitched.

a horizontal row

Use this method to work horizontal rows of colored stitches.

From the back, bring the needle up through the knitted fabric at the base of a stitch. Take the needle under the two loops of the stitch above and back down where it came out, as before. Bring the needle up through the base of the next stitch to the left to work the horizontal row.

sequins

Sequins add lovely sparkle to items such as the sequined earmuffs (see page 16). Here the technique is shown on garter stitch fabric, but you work it in exactly the same way on stockinette (stocking) stitch.

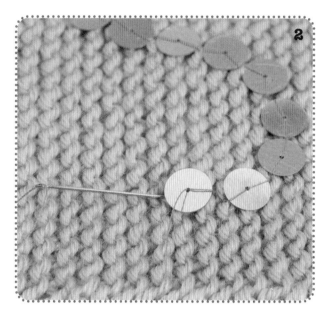

1 Thread a sewing needle with sewing thread. Lay the sequin in position and, from the back of the knitting, bring the needle up through the hole in the middle of the sequin. Take it back down close to the edge.

2 Bring the needle back up through the middle, then back down close to the opposite edge.

Always press knitting before sewing on sequins, as pressing sequins makes them curl and shrivel up.

It might sound time-consuming to sew on sequins by hand, but it's actually quicker than you might think, and the effect is well worth the effort.

yarn information

Here is the fiber and yardage for all the yarns used in this book.

Anchor Artiste Metallic
80% viscose, 20% polyester
Approx 109yds (100m) to a
¾oz (25g) ball

Debbie Bliss Cashmerino Aran
55% merino wool, 33% microfiber, 12% cashmere
Approx 98yds (90m) to a
1¾oz (50g) ball

Debbie Bliss Cathay
50% cotton, 35% viscose microfiber, 15% silk
Approx 109yds (100m) to a 1¾oz (50g) ball

Debbie Bliss Como
90% wool, 10% cashmere
Approx 46yds (42m) to a
1¾oz (50g) ball

Debbie Bliss Donegal Luxury Tweed Chunky
100% wool
Approx 109yds (100m) to a 3½oz (100g) hank

Debbie Bliss Rialto Aran
100% extra-fine merino wool
Approx 87yds (80m) to a 1¾oz (50g) ball

Garthenor 100% Organic Shetland
100% organic Sheltland wool
Approx 179yds (165m) to a 1¾oz (50g) ball

Gedifra Highland Alpaca
50% alpaca, 50% new wool
Approx 44½yds (41m) to a 3½oz (100g) ball

ggh Davos
60% merino wool, 40% acrylic
Approx 96yds (88m) to a 1¾oz (50g) ball

Regia 4-ply
75% wool, 25% polyamide
Approx 230yds (210m) to a 1¾oz (50g) ball

Rowan All Seasons Cotton
60% cotton, 40% microfiber
Approx 98yds (90m) to a 1¾oz (50g) ball

Rowan Baby Alpaca
100% baby alpaca wool
Approx 109yds (100m) to a 1¾oz (50g) ball

Rowan British Sheep Breeds Undyed
100% wool
Approx 120yds (110m) to a 3½oz (100g) ball

Rowan Cashsoft 4-ply
57% extra-fine merino, 33% microfiber, 10% cashmere
Approx 197yds (180m) to a 1¾oz (50g) ball

Rowan Coccoon
80% merino, 20% kid mohair
Approx 126yds (115m) to a 3½oz (100g) ball

Rowan Felted Tweed
50% merino, 25% alpaca, 25% viscose
Approx 191yds (175m) to a 1¾oz (50g) ball

Rowan Kidsilk Haze
70% kid mohair, 30% silk
Approx 229yds (210m) to a ¾oz (25g) ball

Rowan Pure Wool Aran
100% wool
Approx 186yds (170m) to a 3½oz (100g) ball

Rowan Pure Wool DK
100% wool
Approx 137yds (125m) to a 1¾oz (50g) ball

Rowan Shimmer
60% cupro, 40% polyester
Approx 191yds (175m) to a ¾oz (25g) ball

Sirdar Spree
60% cotton, 40% acrylic
Approx 150yds (137m) to a 3½oz (100g) ball

substituting yarn

If you use a yarn that is different to the one suggested, follow these rules before buying.

Firstly, do use a yarn that is the suggested weight, even if you choose a different brand. If you use a worsted weight where the project asks for a bulky weight, you will run into problems.

Secondly, it is the number of yards (metres) of yarn in a ball, not the weight of the ball, that is important. Balls of different brands of yarn, even if they are the same weight, may not contain the same quantity of yarn. So you can't just buy the number of balls the pattern asks for in substitute yarn: you need to do two simple sums.

Given left is the number of yards (metres) per ball for the yarns used in the projects. Multiply the appropriate number of yards (metres) by the number of balls needed to knit the project. This will give you the total number of yards (metres) of yarn you need.

Now check the ball band of your substitute yarn to see how many yards (metres) there are in a ball. Divide the total number of yards (metres) needed by the number in one ball of the substitute yarn and this will tell you how many balls of that yarn you need to buy.

You absolutely must knit a gauge (tension) swatch in the substitute yarn to check that it will achieve the gauge (tension) stated in the pattern.

care of knitwear

Having put time and effort into knitting a project, it's worth looking after it properly.

Many modern yarns can be washed in the washing machine on a special wool cycle. However, if your machine doesn't offer that, then you should hand-wash your knitwear.

Firstly, test that the yarn is colorfast by dipping a corner into warm, soapy water and then squeezing it out with a clean white cloth. If the color stains the cloth, then wash the item in cold water; if not, then use warm water.

Fill the sink with the appropriate water and add soap flakes or wool detergent. Froth up a lather. Put the item in the water and gently squeeze it to push soap into it. Do not leave knitted items to soak for a long time and don't rub the knitting or you risk felting it.

Lift the item out of the water as a single mass to avoid stretching it. Squeeze it to remove excess soapy water, but don't wring it. Fill the sink with clean water and put the item in it. Gently squeeze it to remove the soap suds. Repeat this rinsing until the water stays clear. Lift the item out and squeeze it again to remove excess water.

Lay the item flat on a towel. Roll the towel up and press it firmly to press out as much water as possible. Never, ever wring out a piece of knitwear; you can distort the shape very easily.

To dry the knitting, lay it flat and ease it into shape. Lay it on a flat rack or on a flat surface that has been covered with a towel.

Store your knitting flat, not on a hanger, to avoid stretching it. If you pack your knitwear away for the summer, do put some moth protection in with it. You can buy natural protectors that contain few or no chemicals and don't smell unpleasant.

resources

Lowie can be contacted at info@ilovelowie.com

USA

Anchor crochet yarns
Coats & Clark
Consumer Services
PO Box 12229
Greenville
SC 29612-0229
Tel: +1 800 648 1479
www.coatsandclark.com

Debbie Bliss yarns
Sirdar yarns
Knitting Fever Inc.
PO Box 336
315 Bayview Avenue
Amityville
NY 11701
Tel: +1 516 546 3600
www.knittingfever.com

Gedifra yarns
Regia yarns
Rowan yarns
Westminster Fibers Inc.
165 Ledge Street
Nashua
NH 03063
Tel: +1 800 445 9276
www.westminsterfibers.com

CANADA

Debbie Bliss yarns
Gedifra yarns
Regia yarns
Rowan yarns
Sirdar yarns
Diamond Yarns Ltd
155 Martin Ross Avenue
Unit 3
Toronto
Ontario
M3J 2L9
www.diamondyarn.com

UK

Anchor crochet yarns
Coats Crafts UK
PO Box 22
Lingfield House
Lingfield Point
McMullen Road
Darlington
County Durham
DL1 1YJ
Tel: +44 (0) 1325 394237
www.coatscrafts.co.uk

Debbie Bliss yarns
Designer Yarns Ltd
Units 8-10
Newbridge Industrial Estate
Pitt Street
Keighley
West Yorkshire
BD21 4PQ
Tel: +44 (0) 1535 664222
www.designeryarns.uk.com

Rowan yarns
Gedifra yarns
Rowan Yarns
Tel: +44 (0) 1484 681881
mail@knitrowan.com
www.knitrowan.com

Sirdar yarns
Sirdar Spinning Ltd
Flanshaw Lane
Wakefield
West Yorkshire
WF2 9ND
Tel: +44 (0) 1924 371501
www.sirdar.co.uk

WORLDWIDE

Garthenor yarns
Garthenor Organic Pure Wool
Llanio Road
Tregaron
Wales
SY25 6UR
Tel: (+44) 845 4082437
www.organicpurewool.co.uk
For stockists.

ggh
Mühlenstraße 74
D-25421 Pinneberg
Germany
Tel: 04101 208484
info@ggh-garn.com
www.ggh-garn.de
For stockists.

acknowledgments

Although most of the projects in this book were designed by me, I'd like to thank a few people for their invaluable contribution to *Head to Toe Knits*. Thank you to my publisher, Cindy Richards, who is an inspirational woman and a Lowie fan, and to Kate Haxell, my wonderful editor. Kate is one of the most organized women I've ever met and an invaluable craft expert. Thanks also to my dutiful assistant Hannah, photographer Becky Maynes, hair and makeup artist Hollie Meddings, and to all the models. There are some special ladies without whom there would be no product or patterns with which to fill the book: pattern writer Sue Whiting, knitters Luise, Irene, Ros, Buzz, and Kate, Rowan Yarns for their generous yarn contribution, and pattern checker Marilyn Wilson. I would also like to thank the team at CICO Books, most especially book designer Louise Leffler.

Publisher's acknowledgments
The Fair Isle Earflap Hat (page 18), Roll-neck Capelet (page 32), Wavy Scarf (page 38), Beaded-rib Scarf (page 46), Fair Isle Fingerless Gloves (page 52), and String Bag (page 94) were all designed by Melody Griffiths.

index